This book ... challenges our spiritual mediocrity and spiritual complacency so that we will
be engaged afresh to renew our own spiritual
passion by returning to our first love.

From the Foreword by
TONY EVANS

BILL BRIGHT'S "THE JOY OF KNOWING GOD" SERIES

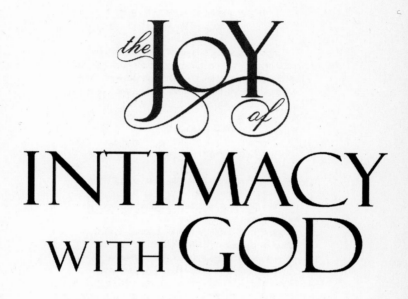

the JOY of
INTIMACY WITH GOD

DR. BILL BRIGHT

The Bible Teacher's Teacher

COOK COMMUNICATIONS MINISTRIES
Colorado Springs, Colorado • Paris, Ontario
KINGSWAY COMMUNICATIONS LTD
Eastbourne, England

Victor® is an imprint of
Cook Communications Ministries,
Colorado Springs, CO 80918
Cook Communications, Paris, Ontario
Kingsway Communications, Eastbourne, England

THE JOY OF INTIMACY WITH GOD
© 2005 by Bill Bright

First Printing, 2005
Printed in the United States of America
1 2 3 4 5 6 7 8 9 10 Printing/Year 09 08 07 06 05

Cover Design: Brand Navigation, LLC

Library of Congress Cataloging-in-Publication Data

Bright, Bill.
    The joy of intimacy with God : rekindling your first love / Bill Bright.
        p. cm. -- (The joy of knowing God series ; bk. 4)
    ISBN 0-7814-4249-4 (pbk.)
    1. Christian life. I. Title. II. Series.

BV4501.3.B7525 2005
248.4--dc22
                                        2004027057

Dedication

GLOBAL FOUNDING PARTNERS

The Bright Media Foundation continues the multifaceted ministries of Bill and Vonette Bright for generations yet unborn. God has touched and inspired the Brights through the ministries of writers through the centuries. Likewise, they wish to pass along God's message in Jesus Christ as they have experienced it, seeking to inspire, train, and transform lives, thereby helping to fulfill the Great Commission each year until our Lord returns.

Many generous friends have prayed and sacrificed to support the Bright Media Foundation's culturally relevant, creative works, in print and electronic forms. The following persons specifically have helped to establish the foundation. These special friends will always be known as Global Founding Partners *of the Bright Media Foundation.*

Bill and Christie Heavener and family

Stuart and Debra Sue Irby and family

Edward E. Haddock Jr., Edye Murphy-Haddock, and the Haddock family

Acknowledgments

It was my privilege to share fifty-four years, six months, and twenty days of married life with a man who loved Jesus passionately and served Him faithfully. Six months before his home going, Bill initiated what has become "The Joy of Knowing God" series. It was his desire to pass along to future generations the insights God had given him that they, too, could discover God's magnificence and live out the wonderful plan He has for their lives.

"The Joy of Knowing God" series is a collection of Bill Bright's top ten life-changing messages. Millions of people around the world have already benefited greatly from these spiritual truths and are now living the exciting Christian adventure that God desires for each of us.

On behalf of Bill, I want to thank the following team that helped research, compile, edit, and wordsmith the manuscripts and audio scripts in this series: Jim Bramlett, Rebecca Cotton, Eric Metaxas, Sheryl Moon, Cecil Price, Michael Richardson, Eric Stanford, and Rob Suggs.

I also want to thank Bill's longtime friends and Campus Crusade associates Bailey Marks and Ted Martin, who carefully reviewed the scripts and manuscripts for accuracy.

Bill was deeply grateful to Bob Angelotti and Don Stillman of Allegiant Marketing Group for their encouragement to produce this series and their ingenuity in facilitating distribution to so many.

A special thanks to Cook Communications and its team of dedicated professionals who partnered with Bright Media Foundation in this venture, as well as to Steve Laube, who brought us together.

Last but not least, I want to express my appreciation to Helmut Teichert, who worked faithfully and diligently in overseeing this team that Bill's vision would be realized, and to John Nill, CEO of Bright Media, who has helped me navigate the many challenges along this journey.

As a result of the hard work of so many, and especially our wonderful Lord's promise of His grace, I trust that multitudes worldwide will experience a greater joy by knowing God and His ways more fully.

With a grateful heart,
MRS. BILL BRIGHT (VONETTE)

Contents

Foreword

The name Bill Bright and godliness seem almost synonymous. The one abiding memory I have of Dr. Bright is his spiritual passion. He would regularly identify himself as "a slave of Jesus Christ." It is because of Bill's fire for Christ that God was able to use him to build the world's largest Christian organization, Campus Crusade for Christ. Because Bill spent countless hours, days, weeks, and even months on the mountain in God's presence, he received the unique privilege and blessing of hearing God's voice.

God used Bill Bright to ignite the spiritual in the hearts and minds of countless millions of people worldwide. Because Bill himself had been ignited by God's consuming fire, everything and everyone he touched became influenced as well.

This book encourages any serious believer to make cultivating their intimacy with God the consuming passion of their lives. It challenges our spiritual mediocrity and spiritual complacency so that we will be engaged afresh to renew our own spiritual passion by returning to our first love.

Bill Bright is among that unique group of believers that has had the privilege of seeing God face-to-face. It's not because he was any better that any other believer—it was just that he pursued intimacy with God as the consuming passion of his life. His insights contained in this work invite us to join in on the greatest adventure of all, namely experiencing the intimate knowledge of God for ourselves.

—TONY EVANS

———————❖———————

"But I have this complaint against you. You don't love me or each other as you did at first! Look how far you have fallen from your first love! Turn back to me again and work as you did at first."

Revelation 2:4–5

———————

PART ONE

Renewing Your Passion for God

I AM CONVINCED THAT NOTHING CAN EVER SEPARATE US FROM HIS LOVE. DEATH CAN'T, AND LIFE CAN'T. THE ANGELS CAN'T, AND THE DEMONS CAN'T. OUR FEARS FOR TODAY, OUR WORRIES ABOUT TOMORROW, AND EVEN THE POWERS OF HELL CAN'T KEEP GOD'S LOVE AWAY. WHETHER WE ARE HIGH ABOVE THE SKY OR IN THE DEEPEST OCEAN, NOTHING IN ALL CREATION WILL EVER BE ABLE TO SEPARATE US FROM THE LOVE OF GOD THAT IS REVEALED IN CHRIST JESUS OUR LORD.

ROMANS 8:38–39

1

Wandering, Not Lost

The greatest power known to man is love. Few would dispute this. You know this truth more deeply than you know anything. And you know that when you are loved, there's a power and freedom in your soul that opens wide new doors of opportunity. Doors of opportunity in your world and in your heart, doors of adventure. That's just a fact.

Somehow when you know you are loved, you're free to reach the highest heights of who you've been created to be. The world seems limitless. And beyond even that, you experience a freedom to love others. You're free to embark on a new road to developing real, refreshing, healthy, and encouraging relationships. And in that experience, you discover a love for life and find life fulfilling, satisfying, and meaningful.

So what is it about love? In 1 Corinthians 13:1–3, Paul explains how important love is to God:

> If I could speak in any language in heaven or on earth but didn't love others, I would only be making meaningless noise like a loud gong or a clanging cymbal. If I had the

gift of prophecy, and if I knew all the mysteries of the future and knew everything about everything, but didn't love others, what good would I be? And if I had the gift of faith so that I could speak to a mountain and make it move, without love I would be no good to anybody. If I gave everything I have to the poor and even sacrificed my body, I could boast about it; but if I didn't love others, I would be of no value whatsoever.

────────❖────────

To love God wholeheartedly is a real challenge.

────────────────

The Bible declares, "God is love" (1 John 4:16). And Jesus, who came to earth as God in the flesh, was and is the personification of love—love incarnate, according to the gospel of John.

And the Bible tells us that the greatest of all the commandments is this: "You must love the LORD your God with all your heart, all your soul, all your mind, and all your strength" (Mark 12:30).

But to love God wholeheartedly is a real challenge. That kind of love doesn't come very easily. How, then, are you to obey God's greatest commandment? How can you ever hope to accomplish that? The answer is simultaneously challenging and simple: Rely on God, who is love. He is the source of all love, even the love with which you love Him back, so to love Him you have to abide in Him and receive His love for you.

According to God's Word, the Christian life is not what you do for Christ but what He does in and through you (Galatians 2:20). So if Jesus, who is the distilled essence of love, lives in and through you as you are surrendered to His will and empowered by His Spirit, you are able to love others, including

Him, with that same divine love—and loving becomes His responsibility.

But how do you do that? This book explains how you can return to—or discover—and maintain your "first love" for God. If you embrace the simple biblical truths presented, you are guaranteed to discover the most exciting adventure the human spirit can ever know. Before you go any further, I invite you to pray the following prayer:

Dear Lord, as I read these pages, please help me to understand and experience afresh your unconditional love for me and show me how to return to my first love for You.

QUALITY TIME

The ultimate reward for having faith in Christ is gaining eternal quality time with Him. That doesn't surprise me, because I know that the presence of God brings inexpressible joy. The incredible news is that this joy is available to you. The apostle Paul assures you of this truth: "Whether we are high above the sky or in the deepest ocean, nothing in all creation will ever be able to separate us from the love of God that is revealed in Christ Jesus our LORD" (Romans 8:39).

Isn't that wonderful? No matter where you are, where you go, what you've done, or what you're doing, you cannot ever be separated from God's love. Ever. And no one—not the president or your parent or a criminal or a pastor—can take it away from you. No matter what.

The only way you can be separated from God is by your own choice. If you feel that you've lost the love you once had for God, or if you've never found it, it's not because He doesn't care for you; it's only because you've turned away from Him. And even that is not enough to separate you from Him! Even if you turn away and wander far, far from Him, He is always right there by you, pursuing you, trying to woo you back. He didn't stop seeking you even when it led Him to die on the cross, and He has never quit trying since.

Consider for a moment the life of Robert Robinson. His is a story of God's ability to turn tragedy into triumph—one of the most moving that I have ever read. Robinson reminds me of so many men and women I have known through the years. Perhaps you will recognize something of yourself in his experience.

Robinson wrote the unforgettable words to the hymn "Come Thou Fount of Every Blessing," one of my favorites. He was a good man who at the age of seventeen placed his trust in Christ through the influence of the great preacher George Whitefield. He later entered the ministry to serve Christ with great love and devotion.

But Robinson was an honest man, too, and he acknowledged a difficult truth about himself: His love for Jesus was deep but not dependable. At times his passion for God waned and the well of his devotion ran dry. Sometimes he felt nothing at all for His Lord. His heart was "prone to wander."

This cold truth troubled Robinson. As he grappled with it, he began to write out his thoughts and feelings, and finally produced a timeless hymn. "Come Thou Fount" is an autobiographical story of a man so unworthy, so unfaithful, yet always forgiven and welcomed home to the loving arms of his Lord.

As time moved on and Robinson grew older, he wandered farther and farther from God. His actions and attitudes began to darken, and he came to feel that the distance between God and himself had become too great to be reconciled. Sin and corruption had taken root in his life. How could he ever look into the eyes of Jesus again? Robert Robinson was a miserable man, consumed by the grief of his own guilt. With the restless heart of Jonah, of the Prodigal Son, and of every guilt-ridden soul, he took to the road. Maybe some distant land would hold the cure. Maybe he could somehow leave his self-condemnation behind.

One day, a young woman, who was filled with the joy of Christ and who could talk of nothing else, sat across from him in a stagecoach. Robinson, of course, would have chosen any other topic available. But he was a captive audience; he could not, obviously, leap out of a moving carriage. So he resigned himself to a discussion of spiritual matters. In those days, people used hymnals as devotional books, and this young woman had such a volume in her lap. She said, "Sir, I'd like your opinion of one of these hymns—one that has been such a powerful influence in my life." And she handed the hymnal across to him.

You are guaranteed to discover the most exciting adventure the human spirit can ever know.

Robinson looked at the page and found himself confronted by his own words. His throat ran dry and he could think of nothing to say. He tried to hand the book back to her. But the young lady persisted, assuming he must be as moved by the words to "Come Thou Fount" as she was. Maybe that was the reason for the sudden wetness in his eyes, the great tears sliding down his face. But slowly the realization dawned on her that she was looking into the face of a tortured soul.

Robinson saw that she knew the truth. He began to nod slowly, then the words finally followed: "I am the man who wrote that hymn," he said. "Many years ago. I'd give anything to experience that joy again—*anything*."

The woman was shocked. She looked down at the page and saw the name of the poet who was sitting across from her: *Robert Robinson*. His life story was written in the ink below her, and his portrait was painted in the tears of the man before her.

The young lady pointed to the lines he knew so well. She began to speak gently about the "streams of mercy, never ceasing" that were still deep enough to drown his tears. She showed him there were no seasons too lengthy, no distance too great for the love of God to find him, comfort him, and bring him home again.

That day, Robert Robinson, broken and defeated, rediscovered the love he had left behind. I can imagine the joy he felt, because in my own life, that first love is everything.

HOLDING ON FOR DEAR LIFE

Quite often people ask me, "How can I pray for you?" I always answer them the same way. I ask them to pray that wherever I go and whatever I do, I will never leave my first love. Ever since I was a young Christian, astounded by the power of God's presence and overwhelmed with His love, I have made it my first priority to hold on for dear life to my intimate, personal relationship with Him. Through my more than fifty busy years with my Lord, there have been countless problems, challenges, and opportunities. I knew in the very beginning that simply serving God was not enough. I longed to possess a heart overflowing with love and praise for my Lord. If I failed to maintain my first love, my disobedience would undermine all I hold dear. I knew that in time I would disintegrate as a believer, a husband, a father, a person, and a businessman. My first love for God—Father, Son, and Holy Spirit—is everything to me.

For me, the price of maintaining that devotion has been daily submission. As partners in marriage, Vonette and I, as a practice, begin each morning and end each evening on our knees in prayer, acknowledging the Lord Jesus as our Master,

> *No matter what your circumstances, what you may have done, or how long you may have rebelled, God's heart of love remains open to you.*

Savior, and King. The Bible teaches that the living Christ dwells in every believer, so we ask Him each day to walk around in our bodies, think with our minds, love with our hearts, speak with our lips, and continue "seeking and saving" the lost through our efforts. All day long, I seek to walk and talk with my Savior no matter what the business of the day might be. If I can cling to His love from one moment to the next, I know I will never leave it. In this way I seek to "pray continually" (1 Thessalonians 5:17 NIV) as I "practice the presence of God" (see Brother Lawrence, *Practicing the Presence of God*).

In these recent times I have faced new medical challenges: incurable fibrosis of the lungs, cancer, and diabetes. When I pour out my prayers to God and read His Word, I can no longer fall to my knees quite so easily. If I did, the Lord knows I would have trouble rising again. But He understands that. He cares more about a sturdy heart than wobbly knees.

I see doctors regularly and have had my share of surgeries. I now depend upon the help of a wonderful apparatus almost twenty-four hours each day to help me breath the oxygen I need. As Job once said, "The LORD gave me everything I had, and the LORD has taken it away. Praise the name of the LORD!" (Job 1:21). Yes, He has given me so much, all through the years and right up to the present. But the greatest gift of all, in those wonderful words that Robert Robinson gave us, is a heart that can be tuned to sing his praise. Much of my mobility has been taken away. I have lost over half of my breathing capacity and much of the energy to do all that I would like to do for Him. At the age of eighty, I have far fewer days before me than I have behind me. But God has left me with the one thing that I treasure most: the ability to love Him with my first love, and to praise Him with my mind and emotions every moment that I live on this earth. By the grace of God, I will never take leave of my first love for Him.

WE'RE INSEPARABLE

I do not want to give you the impression that I am perfect—my heart is not as pure as I would like it to be. No one is perfect but Jesus. I have the same traces of sin and rebellion within me that all people must confront. Daily my flesh wars against my spirit (Galatians 5:16–17). My heart is prone to wander just as yours is. It requires daily vigilance to protect my spirit from leaving my first love. But it is more than worth the struggle and daily discipline. God's love is so strengthening and so refreshing. I can face any medical problem that may lie before me. I can face the prospect of death itself with joy. But I could never face the possibility of separation from that perfect love of God that sustains my spirit. I take great comfort from God's wonderful assurance recorded in Romans 8:38–39:

> I am convinced that nothing can ever separate us from his
> love. Death can't, and life can't. The angels can't, and the

demons can't. Our fears for today, our worries about tomorrow, and even the powers of hell can't keep God's love away. Whether we are high above the sky or in the deepest ocean, nothing in all creation will ever be able to separate us from the love of God that is revealed in Christ Jesus our Lord.

So you see, absolutely nothing can separate you from that first love. Not even the angels and demons can come between God and you. Not even death itself can provide a barrier. The only thing that can take away your first love is your own spirit, prone to wander.

First Corinthians 13:13 tells us of "three things that will endure—faith, hope, and love—and the greatest of these is love." My faith will be fulfilled one day when I see Jesus face to face. All my hopes will be complete. My love for God, and His love for me, will endure forever, from now right into eternity. The Bible says it is the greatest thing of all. I would not want to leave that even for an instant.

How's your spirit today? Have you wandered? Have you left your first love? How would you describe the state of your affection for Him today? Can you remember how it felt on the day you first met Him? How far have you wandered from the place where He wants you to be? What will it take for you to return to that first love that He wants you to experience as a way of life?

Those are some of the questions I pray you can answer by reading this book.

Jesus commands you to love God with all your mind, heart, soul, and strength. As Paul has shown, there is no distance of time or space that can keep you from His wonderful love. You may run halfway around the world, and you may hide from God for the best years of your life. No matter what your circumstances, what you may have done, or how long you may have rebelled, God's heart of love remains open to you. You *can* go home—home to the arms of the Father who will never stop waiting for you with His love, never stop seeking to restore the joy and wonder of your salvation.

TAKE AND SEAL IT

If, as a believer, your heart is prone to wander, if your well of devotion has run dry, if you have somehow, through the busyness of life and the maze of challenges and relationships, left your first love—He's waiting for you.

As sinful and rebellious as you are, you're still the object of God's love. As a human being filled with disobedience, you deserve nothing but punishment and eternal banishment from His holy presence; yet God himself, deliberately as an act of His great love, endured the punishment of the cross so you could avoid it. He submitted himself to the most painful and degrading execution men could possibly inflict just so He could offer His rescue from the kingdom of darkness to the very agents of His suffering. His love pursues you forever, and the cross is the ultimate picture of that.

Even today, I feel deep emotion when I consider all that His death on the cross means to me. It might have been me at the foot of that cross, pounding iron nails into His wrists. Even so, He would offer me no less love, no less forgiveness. As John put it, "This is real love" (1 John 4:10). The greatest devotion I could muster can never compare.

If you do not know the Lord Jesus Christ personally, my prayer is that this book will help you make the most wonderful discovery possible for time and eternity. Then, when your heart is united with the heart of God, be sure to bind them together for the glory of God and your eternal blessing. Mr. Robinson's song put it so beautifully:

Prone to wander, Lord, I feel it.
Prone to leave the God I love.
Here's my heart, Lord, take and seal it.
Seal it for Thy courts above.

Through the years I have learned a lot about surgery, and that verse describes an operation I recommend for each of us: the sealing of our hearts to the great, loving heart of God. Would you like to have that happen in your life? Would you like to know that you are in the presence of a wonderful, loving Father once and for all, inseparable forever?

It will happen if you truly want it to. Today you can discover how the Lord can seal your heart. You will have the marvelous assurance that His wonderful, all-surpassing, unconditional love will never let you go—and from that moment on, you will never let *Him* go. Your first love will become your ultimate and final one, and the love of all your days, hours, and moments for all time and eternity.

THIS IS REAL LOVE. IT IS NOT THAT WE LOVED GOD,
BUT THAT HE LOVED US AND SENT HIS SON AS A
SACRIFICE TO TAKE AWAY OUR SINS.

1 JOHN 4:10

2

Transformed by Love

The love of God took me entirely by surprise. It was the last thing that I expected, and the only thing that could have completely captured my devotion.

In 1945, I was a young businessman in Hollywood with the whole world before me. I was working long hours, chasing the American dream of building my own business and a financial fortune. Frankly, I was off to a very promising start. Business was going well. But from my first day in California, something unexpected and unusual began to happen to me—something that can be accounted for only by the sovereign, invisible, loving hand of God.

I had just arrived in Los Angeles and was on my way to Pasadena. I happened to pick up a hitchhiker by the side of the road. (I should mention that I do not recommend hitchhiking or picking up riders in today's dangerous times, but no one considered it risky sixty years ago. It was simply an act of kindness.) This particular hitchhiker was a friendly young man who kindly invited me to spend the night in the home of Dawson and Lila Trotman. Dawson was the founder of the great

Christian movement The Navigators, of which my passenger was a member. Later that evening, I was invited to the home of Charles E. Fuller for a birthday party for his son Dan (many years later I was privileged to be the best man in Dan and Ruth's wedding). Can you imagine—here I was, an unbeliever, spending my first night in Los Angeles in the homes of two of the greatest Christian leaders of the twentieth century! How can one explain such a remarkable experience? In retrospect, I can see that God was simply answering the prayer of my saintly mother who asked that God would watch over me and direct my steps.

> *They had a special quality about them—a dynamic, positive charisma that I had never seen in such abundance.*

Over a year passed and I was invited to visit one of the city's finest churches, the First Presbyterian Church of Hollywood. It had a vibrant young adult group that immediately attracted me. As I attended their meetings and classes, I was amazed at what I observed among the members. They had a special quality about them—a dynamic, positive charisma that I had never seen in such abundance. Church had not meant much to me before this time, but these people had an infectious spirit about them. I became more and more involved with the group until I was forced, over a period of months, to confront my own spiritual condition.

I looked for my old, neglected Bible, which my mother had given me when I was a young teenager. Wiping off the dust, I began to study the life and words of Jesus with new interest. A godly mother had raised me; I had been to church and had heard a few sermons. But the words of the Gospels seemed brand new, as if I had never heard them before. They absorbed me and captivated my spirit. Over a period of months, as I listened to sermons and read God's Word, it was as if Jesus stepped right out of that Holy Book and commanded my full and complete devotion. I was convinced that He was the most incredible and remarkable person to ever walk this earth.

My teacher at church, Dr. Henrietta Mears, was another "chance" acquaintance whom God sent to me at this crucial time. Her passion for Jesus not only influenced my life, but led to the founding of a publishing house, a conference retreat center, Bible study materials still in use today, and a legacy of hundreds of men and women all over the world—including Billy Graham—whose faiths were ignited when touched by her ministry.

Dr. Mears and my pastor, Dr. Louis Evans, helped me understand that Jesus is actually much more than the greatest Man who ever lived. He is God incarnate, walking among mankind so that I could know and love Him in the fullest sense. Along with my mother, Dr. Mears and Dr. Evans showed me that Christ is Lord of all; they demonstrated the complete love and devotion a Christian ought to have for Him.

> *I went to California to pursue a career, but when I got there, Christ pursued me.*

WHEN LOVE IS REAL

I went to California to pursue a career, but when I got there, Christ pursued me. I believe that He sovereignly put me in certain places and among specific people for His purposes. It took the right combination of events for me to finally see Jesus for who He really is. I had grown up doing my daily chores on the family ranch, listening to my mother sing hymns with quiet contentment as she worked. I had seen her rise early every day to pray and study God's Word, no matter how busy she was. But now, as a young believer, I finally understood the joy that lay beneath those melodies that filled her heart. I could finally see why she was so eager to open that leather-bound Book each morning and evening to talk with her Creator.

My father and mother had been married for thirty-five years in a home that was divided—he was not a believer. After I met Jesus, my father became my number-one prayer target. My father prayed with me and received Christ as his Savior approximately a year after He became my Lord. My parents lived for thirty-five more years with Christ as Lord of their marriage, a miraculous difference. We had many rich and rewarding times together. Both my mother and my father went to be with the Lord at the age of ninety-three.

> God is love ... *those are the three most beautiful words ever written.*

The more I learned about Jesus, the greater my love for Him grew. First John, a letter as powerful as it is concise, taught me much about this subject of love:

> Anyone who does not love does not know God—for God is love. God showed how much he loved us by sending his only Son into the world so that we might have eternal life through him. This is real love. It is not that we loved God, but that he loved us and sent his Son as a sacrifice to take away our sins.
>
> 1 JOHN 4:8–10

It is so simple! How had I missed it in the past? *God is*

love! To me, those are the three most beautiful words ever written. They are the three words that turn the world upside-down, that transform all sadness into joy and all defeat into victory. No other three words could be so simple, so profound, so powerful. *God is love.*

John also says that it is not a matter of trying to love God. It all begins with Him. It must be true, because I know that I am incapable of loving as I should. I am able to love Him or to love anyone else only because He took the initiative; *He* first loved (1 John 4:19). He loved man from the beginning of creation and, through the long years, felt deep sorrow and anger when we continued to rebel against Him and reject His laws. Finally, moved by a love and compassion I will never understand, He personally came and rescued me—and you!—once and for all at the cross.

KEEP THE FIRE BURNING

I studied the words of 1 John as a newborn Christian. I had never considered myself a "sinner," as I might have defined it as a young man back home in Coweta, Oklahoma. But now I saw things differently. Now I understood that my sins were just as terrible as those of the men who crucified my Lord. God had done so much for me, and I had done less than nothing for Him.

Money and business had been my gods. Success and fame had been my altar of worship. And yet He had loved me enough to pursue me, to place me among all these loving people, from my very first night in Southern California.

"God is love," writes John, "and all who live in love live in God, and God lives in them. And as we live in God, our love grows more perfect" (1 John 4:16–17).

Those simple words described the life for which I yearned. I decided that I would no longer live in greed. I would, with God's help, live in love. According to this verse, succeeding in this goal would be the proof that God lived within me. I would not stray from the love of God but strive to see it grow "more perfect." It would be reflected in my selfless devotion to God and to others.

John Calvin, the great reformer from Geneva, used the symbol of a hand holding a flaming heart. The inscription read, "My heart I give Thee, Lord, eagerly and sincerely." When I first caught fire for Christ and as my love for Him grew, some friends and I claimed that image for our own. We called ourselves the Fellowship of the Burning Heart and pledged to make ourselves totally expendable for God.

Ever since then, I have tried to keep my heart as an eternal flame of passion for God and His purposes. One Sunday afternoon in 1951, Vonette and I, after much prayer, "signed away" our lives, our future, and everything we owned or would ever own to Christ. Next to the moment of my salvation, this was the most important and liberating day of my life. We uncondi-tionally turned over to our loving Father, our holy God and Savior, every possession, goal, or concern of our present or future. It was a contract with

He has been more than faithful to keep His promises every moment of every day.

God to be bond-slaves to the only Master who could ever love and care for us. We were inspired to be His slaves since He had become a slave for all people (Philippians 2:7). Also Paul and Timothy in Philippians 1:1 proclaimed themselves to be slaves of Jesus, as did Peter, James, and Jude (2 Peter 1:1; James 1:1; Jude 1).

I can say only that, in the more than fifty years that have followed, He has been more than faithful to keep His promises every moment of every day. Vonette and I have very few possessions. We do not even own the home in which we live or the cars we drive, but He graciously provides every need as He promised to do in Philippians 4:19.

God makes His wonderful, boundless love available to you every moment of every day. How could you live without it? How could your first love for Him ever slip away when His love is so perfect and so faithful? And yet I realize that it is a genuine danger for every Christian.

Most true believers in Christ can point to a time when their hearts were on fire for Him. They loved Christ with a passion that no one could help but notice. Their hearts were on fire for Him. His love had transformed them from the inside out. But somehow, for many reasons and without intending to, many Christians let the flames of love and devotion to God die down to glowing embers, a wisp of smoke, and ashes.

Few things are sadder than the ashes of a burned-out devotion.

Few things are sadder than the ashes of a burned-out devotion.

HANDS AND HEART

How do Christians let this happen? One reason may be that it is easier, in some ways, to be a Martha than a Mary. The story of these two sisters is found in Luke 10:38–42, and it has always fascinated me. Those who have known me well will tell you I, like Martha, am a "doer" by nature; I favor action and accomplishment. I like to get things done. But doing work for God is precisely how I might avoid God himself.

I think Martha may have thought that way. Let us try to see her point of view. She lived in Bethany, not far from Jerusalem. One day Jesus came in with all of His entourage—disciples and friends—chattering, joking, arguing. With her home filled with guests, Martha immediately fell into the role of hostess— cooking, cleaning, and serving. This was the way a first-century woman showed her devotion, and no one would have faulted her actions. It was not Martha but Mary, her sister, whose behavior might have been called into question. Mary sat right at Jesus' feet, where a true disciple would traditionally take a position. Other guests might have used chairs, but a serious disciple sat at the Master's feet.

Still, Martha busily prepared dinner. Then she did a very human thing. She approached Jesus and said, "Lord, doesn't it seem unfair to you that my sister just sits here while I do all the work? Tell her to come and help me" (v. 40).

Jesus replied with the words I need to hear, and to hear attentively: "My dear Martha, you are so upset over all these details! There is really only one thing worth being concerned about. Mary has discovered it—and I won't take it away from her" (vv. 41–42). Jesus knew the writing of Moses well, but He could have had the Book of Ecclesiastes in mind when He responded to Martha.

I believe Martha had a good heart but a *busy* heart. You know the temptation to become so busy with the whirlwind of service that you take leave of the passion that first inspired that service. Soon the conflicts and challenges begin to upset and distract you, and they obviously did that to Martha. In no way is Jesus saying that you should neglect everyday responsibilities. But you cannot let those things become diversions from the "one thing worth being concerned about." As Jesus taught, "seek first his kingdom and his righteousness, and all these things will be given to you as well" (Matthew 6:33 NIV). If you do anything, it should be an expression of your love for Him. But if what you do is not an expression of that love, it's far worse than if you did nothing all.

Jesus stressed this truth often. He underlined it again in the story of the sower and the seeds in Matthew 13. The farmer threw out his seeds, and they fell in various places that determined whether they took root and grew. Some of the seeds fell among thorns. After telling the story, Jesus explained "the thorny ground represents those who hear and accept the Good News, but all too quickly the message is crowded out by the cares of this life and the lure of wealth, so no crop is produced" (Matthew 13:22).

> *If what you do is not an expression of that love, it's far worse than if you did nothing all.*

If you find yourself chasing success, fame, the praise and applause of others, and so many concerns, you may forget the one thing about which you should be concerned. But you can avoid those thorns! You can sit at the Master's feet and listen carefully to His voice. Then your love for Him will linger.

My mother had the hands of Martha and the heart of Mary. She stayed busy all day with the work of a rancher's wife and mother of seven children. But all the while, she was humming songs of worship and praise. I think she had "discovered it"— and Jesus never allowed her to lose it.

What about you? Have you become busy with the details of life and left your passion somewhere along the way?

Consider a group of Christians from the first century who had that experience. They fell head over heels in love with God and made a powerful impact upon a wicked city. Then somehow they left their first love.

A Love Left Behind

In the book of Revelation, the Lord Jesus speaks directly to seven prominent churches of the first century. He greets each of them, except for the church at Laodicea, with a "pat on the back," a word of commendation for work well done. Then He gets down to business; He tells five what must be improved.

The first of these churches is located in the great city of Ephesus. It sounds as if the church had more than its share of "Marthas"—tireless servants who had busied their hands but lost their hearts.

> I know all the things you do. I have seen your hard work and your patient endurance ... You have patiently suffered for me without quitting. But I have this complaint against you. You don't love me or each other as you did at first! Look how far you have fallen from your first love! Turn back to me again and work as you did at first. If you don't, I will come and remove your lampstand from its place among the churches.
>
> REVELATION 2:2–5

Look closely at these words because they are vitally important for everyone who knows and loves God. The Lord is saying, "You have served Me well. You have suffered for Me patiently. You have endured over the long run. Good job! These are wonderful accomplishments. But I must tell you that something troubles Me deeply. I'm referring to your love for Me and for one another."

Those words may startle you. But He continues, "Your love is not what it once was. You have left it behind! Don't you recall how things used to be? Don't you remember the time when your hearts were ablaze with love for Me—and how that love overflowed into your relationships with each other? Oh, how you've fallen from those lofty heights! But there is good news: You can set things right again—back to how they were!"

Come home—that is the message. The original language, by the way, does not say that those believers have *lost* their first love; it says they have *left* it or *forsaken* it as an act of their will. I hope you can see what a difference that makes. You do not "lose" your love for a spouse, for a friend, or for Jesus Christ. You walk away from it. If you say you've lost something, it almost sounds as if it is just an unfortunate occurrence that is nobody's fault—something you can lose in the same way you would misplace your car keys. But you are responsible to take hold of the love God has poured out upon you. It is up to you to cling to it and never let it go. If you wander, God says, "Come home. You're welcome here."

MIND, HEART, SOUL, AND STRENGTH

The Ephesians, however, had not done that. They had left their first love behind, and now God is inviting them—and you—to come home.

In the fifth verse, Jesus reveals the path that leads homeward to the place no one should ever have left. These steps will lead you home:

Remember (2:5a)

Remorse (2:5a)

Repent (2:5b)

Resume (2:5c)

In its simplest terms, the path back to your first love is this illustrated by the following chart:

What You Do	What You Use	What Jesus Calls It
You think. *(Remember)*	Mind	"Look how far ..."
You feel. *(Remorse)*	Heart	"... you have fallen from your first love!"
You change. *(Repent)*	Soul	"Turn back to me again."
You work. *(Resume)*	Strength	"And work as you did at first."

God's plan, as you would expect, is a perfect one. It uses your mind, heart, soul, and strength—everything about you—to bring you back into His presence. He wants *all* of you so that you may experience all of *Him.* It is no coincidence that Jesus said the greatest commandment is this: "You must love the Lord your God with *all* your heart, *all* your soul, *all* your mind, and *all* your strength" (Mark 12:30).

Jesus also taught that the second commandment followed naturally from the first one: "Love your neighbor as yourself" (v. 31). Notice that Jesus said to the Ephesians, "You don't love me *or each other* as you did at first" (Revelation 2:4). Love for people is the overflow that comes from a love for God. You absolutely cannot love the Lord with all your mind, heart, soul, and strength without having that love overflow into your other relationships—beginning with your nearest neighbors, your spouse and children, your parents and grandparents, aunts, uncles, and cousins. It works in both directions, too; when you lose the joy of God, you will begin to lose the joy of people.

Where are you today in that regard? Are you in a state of loving unity with the people important to you? If you're struggling with relationships in your family, in your workplace, or in your established friendships, the first place you should check is how you're getting along with God.

You love God (*or* reject God) with every part of your being—mind, heart, soul, and strength. When Jesus spoke with His disciples in His most intimate teaching, in the Upper Room, He called it *abiding* or *remaining* in Him: "Remain in me, and I will remain in you." He also says, "For a branch cannot produce fruit if it is severed from the vine, and you cannot be fruitful apart from me" (John 15:4).

Abiding in Christ is the deepest meaning of maintaining your first love. As you remain in Him with every part of your being, you are as fully dependent upon Him as a branch is upon a tree or vine. If you remain, you grow more healthy and begin to bear fruit. Your relationships become richer. Your work becomes more excellent. And others come to know the Lord because they see the evidence of God in you.

RESULTS

When you have reclaimed your first love for God, you experience *revival*.

In 1994 I began one of the most wonderful spiritual journeys of my life. Following our Lord's example of fasting, God led me to fast and pray for forty days for national and world revival and for the fulfillment of the Great Commission. He has led me to continue this blessed discipline each year since. After my fourth forty-day fast, God's Spirit showed me that such a fast is a vital part of the Great Commission. When He said in Matthew 28:20, "Teach these new disciples to obey all the commands I have given you," that would include the practice of fasting. No other discipline meets the conditions of 2 Chronicles 7:14 like fasting and prayer. And nothing can accelerate your return to "first love" like fasting and prayer.

This is how revivals begin, and for years I have fasted and prayed that I might live to see revival among believers within our nation and throughout the world. As a matter of fact, historical revivals and spiritual awakenings have always been marked by some signifying godly trait. I believe that when we experience the next world revival, it will be marked by a revival of *love*. This was the assurance that the Holy Spirit gave me during my first forty-day fast—that He would send a revival and it would be a revival of love.

Jesus also refers to an additional event: After renewing our first love, we will receive a *reward* (Revelation 2:7).

Remember. Remorse. Repent. Resume. We will explore each of these steps together, and by the grace of God your devotion for Him will catch fire once again, rising to a mighty flame. Those around you will move closer just to warm their hearts and hands in the glow of your restored (or new) first love for God.

3

Remembrance: Reliving Your First Love

When you feel spiritually dry and empty, and God's voice seems to have been silent for a great period, it helps to turn to your memories—memories of God's past goodness. They're crucial and irreplaceable. Throughout the Bible, God calls His people to cling to their history and draw strength from it. Scripture says, "Remember the height from which you have fallen!" (Revelation 2:5a NIV).

Remembrance is the work of the mind. If your heart has grown cold, you must rely upon your mind. You may stop feeling, but you never stop thinking. So the mind is the best place to stir up the embers that will warm your heart once again.

Remembering shocks you into realization: Things have changed! You have loosened your hold on the greatest thing life has to offer. In remembering, you feel deep remorse that you have deliberately left home, your first love. The reflection of the mind will lead to the sorrow of the heart. When you have fully come to terms with the truth of it, only then will you be moved to repent. You internally change your focus from yourself toward God. Finally, you begin to do those things of first importance again.

I must point out, of course, that those who have never known God will have no such memories. If you have never received our Lord Jesus Christ and walked with Him, you cannot know the beauty and grace of that marvelous experience. You will feel a longing instead. You will have an awareness of your failures and limitations as a human being. God's Spirit is beckoning to you, drawing you to Himself. If you are experiencing a deep desire in your heart to turn from your sins, as we call our spiritual failures, and to experience God's wonderful love and forgiveness for the first time, be assured that He is waiting for you with open arms.

But if sometime in the past you have known God intimately and have lost the intensity of your passion for Him, you can be sure that He is waiting for you to return. In the worst of times, when you cannot seem to hear His voice or feel His touch, you still have an amazing resource. You can consult those incredible filing cabinets in the human mind—your memories. Think about something you have enjoyed over the years: Christmas, Thanksgiving, Easter, springtime, football season, vacation in a very special place. When you take the time to relive your memories of these things, your spirit seems to catch a second wind. You feel your excitement begin to build. It is not difficult to develop a frame of mind that feels like a cool, refreshing wind.

DOUBLY LOVED

I *really* hit the jackpot! I found my heavenly love and my earthly love during approximately the same period. Even as I was making the wonderful discovery of God's goodness, He showed me that Vonette Zachary was the right life partner for me.

I remember sitting across the dinner table from her the

night I proposed, after taking her to the Red Bud Ball at Texas Women's University where she was a sophomore. I told her all about my ambitious plans for life and how they all included her. I was living in Hollywood, a city filled with beautiful women. But in my eyes, none of them could compare with the beauty of Vonette, inside and outside. Her positive response thrilled my heart. Together we committed ourselves to Christ and to our relationship, and we've never left that love for God or for each other—even after fifty years of marriage.

If you have ever been engaged to be married, you know what it is like to be utterly devoted to someone. Vonette and I were separated by many miles, she in Texas and I in California, but I kept a constant stream of special-delivery letters, flowers, candy, and long-distance phone calls flowing in her direction. I did everything I could possibly think of to impress and woo her because I wanted her to see how serious I was. I wanted her to feel the same way about me as I felt about her. Romantic love surprises us as it brings out creativity we never knew we had. And there is a deep longing as well; I can remember eagerly anticipating the time when we could actually be united in marriage, never to be separated.

I was experiencing these same feelings toward God. I wanted *Him* to be with me for the rest of my life, too. I did everything I could to please Him, and devoted much time to prayer and the study of His Word. I spent five years at Princeton and Fuller Theological Seminaries because I desired to learn more about Jesus. I yearned to know Him better and to be drawn closer to His great, loving heart, just as I yearned to spend time with Vonette.

LOVE REJUVENATED

Our first love for God works under many of the same dynamics as a good marriage. Meeting God for the first time is euphoric. There is a "honeymoon period" of faith in which loving God comes so easily and so naturally. With every new morning you are eager to meet with Him in prayer and to study His Word. You're aware of His presence wherever you go. But over the long years that follow, too often the thrill fades. The initial joy slowly dissipates—until, without being aware of it, you discover that you have left your first love.

Young, immature euphoria needs to deepen into something far greater, far more rewarding to you and honoring to God. When you sometimes fail Him, you must confess your sin, repent, and correct your ways. In doing so you ultimately build a deep, abiding intimacy. Joy is still there, but you become more focused on loving God by serving Him. You experience your Lord most deeply and you please Him most fully when you're doing the things He wants you to do.

In His Word, Jesus frequently calls the Church—you and me—His *bride*. The joy of a perfect marriage, great as it may be, is only a dim reflection of the deepest and most intense pleasure of all: knowing God in an intimate, loving, personal way.

Vonette and I find that when we relive our first love for each other, we enhance the memory of those early sparks. We talk over the long-ago days when I courted her through the mail, when we had the unique enjoyment of talking about things for the first time, each of us learning how the other thought and felt. We try to recapture some of the eagerness, creativity, and playfulness of those times, and it is amazing how our love is rejuvenated.

Vonette and I love to please each other, and we love to serve God together. After half a century, that has been our life: pleasing Him by loving each other, and pleasing each other by loving Him. It is the most complete joy we know. Recently, while visiting at the home of dear friends, Pearl and Jack Galpin, we read these words from a lovely plaque: "Lord, help me to see thee more clearly, love thee more dearly, follow thee more nearly." These words have become our earnest prayer.

Just recently we had two of our grandchildren, Kellor and Noel, visiting us in our Orlando home. Vonette and I enjoyed watching them play a game of Dominoes. After they returned home, I challenged Vonette to a game. We had not played Dominoes for many years. I must say, we enjoyed our time together in this way with much laughter and fun.

Frankly, that happens too seldom with our loved ones and with our Lord. We fall into ruts of stale habits. Ruts are those dusty, well-worn ditches that have been described as "coffins with the ends knocked out." We dare not let our relationships grow stale and dusty. We need that special spark of newness and refreshment, and a wonderful way to find it is by reliving the better times we have shared.

We need to stop and remember—and relive.

STROLLING DOWN MEMORY LANE

How can you remember the height from which you have fallen when it comes to your relationship with God?

Begin by simply taking the time to reflect. If you once experienced that kind of a love life with the Savior, deliberately contemplate that time. Call on all the resources of your memory and try to recapture a mental snapshot of what that first love was like. Where and when did you first meet the

Lord? How did it feel? What were the first things you did? Make a list of the people who knew you then; ask them what they observed in your expressions, words, and actions.

Think about how God changed your life when you experienced your first love for Him. What habits were a part of your life? How did you conduct your prayer life? What sections of the Bible meant the most to you? I suggest that you take a sheet of paper, draw a line down the middle, and make a simple chart. On the left side, write words or phrases describing your feelings and experiences at the time of your first love. Simple things will do. On the right side, note how that item has changed, if it has.

When you do this exercise, you may see evidence of slow erosion—small, seemingly insignificant compromises in your original commitment to God. These may not be obvious, consequential matters. Certainly you may still be serving God faithfully, just as those in Ephesus did. You may have excellent church attendance. You may be reading your Bible daily. But do not be surprised if you find that the marks of your early passion have slowly faded and disappeared, often without your noticing.

Then, after you've reflected on that, I invite you to talk to God about your observations. Even if you do not feel His presence, speak to Him as you would any friend or loved one, for He is closer to you than your own heart. If it will help you to focus your thoughts, go to a private place and speak aloud to God. If you feel emotional, let the tears flow. It's cleansing. Be completely candid with God; He knows you better than anyone does, even better than you do.

You may also want to begin a "First Love" journal and write out your prayers to God every day. It will become a diary of your journey back to His loving arms.

4

Remorse: Realizing the Loss

As you remember what your first love was like, you gain perspective—you come to understand the height from which you have fallen. That, my friend, will engage the emotions—your heart. You will feel deep remorse, or what Paul calls "godly sorrow." After sending a letter of rebuke to the Corinthians, Paul wrote:

> Now I am happy, not because you were made sorry, but because your sorrow led you to repentance. For you became sorrowful as God intended and so were not harmed in any way by us. Godly sorrow brings repentance that leads to salvation and leaves no regret, but worldly sorrow brings death.
>
> 2 CORINTHIANS 7:9–10, NIV

When you hurt deeply as you realize that the love has gone out of your faith, that is godly sorrow. The right kind of sorrow is a "good pain" because it leads us to repentance. This is when joy occurs.

GOOD PAIN

Let me assure you of one thing: God is not hiding from you. If you feel the pain of separation from Him, that is a *good* pain—the unmistakable sign of His presence. I do not like to submit to the dentist's drill any more than I imagine you do, but I've learned some interesting lessons in that chair. The dental surgeon tells me that in the case of a root canal, a cluster of nerves must be removed. While this gives me wonderful relief from an aching tooth, my dentist is highly reluctant to perform the procedure. He knows that the tooth itself will now become dry, no longer nourished daily by the flow of healthy blood. In time, dryness will make the tooth brittle and in danger of breaking (that is why the dentist must "crown" the tooth). A living tooth is sensitive; the pain tells you it is alive. A dead tooth simply dries out and gives off no signals.

You may feel dry, but it is a yearning for life.

As long as you feel an ache in your spirit, you know there is healthy life there. God is near—the discomfort is His way of telling you that your relationship needs special care. You may feel dry, but it is not the dryness of death—it is a yearning for life. You may feel pain, but you can know that your pain is fully shared by your Creator and Savior. For every tear you shed, He sheds one along with you. He longs for you to draw closer and feel His comfort. His love, as we've seen, is the greatest and most profound thing in the universe. He is drawing you back to your first love for Him.

Sometimes it is necessary to move through a period of sorrow to reach the destination of joy. As remembrance brings

you to remorse, you are ready for the next step. Take heart—
the best is yet to come!

Near Death

The television program *Dateline* ran a heartbreaking story
recently. Fortunately it did have a happy ending. The
show reported on a very young Canadian girl named Erika, no
more than two years old. On the frigid evening of February 24,
2001, she was sleeping beside her mother. But she climbed out
of the bed, wandered out the front door, and spent a freezing
night outdoors, unprotected.

When her mother found her, the girl appeared to be
frozen. Her legs and body were stiff and there were no signs of
life. The frantic mother thought her daughter was dead, but
she rushed her to the hospital. There, by the grace of God, the
skilled medical personnel worked a miracle and revived Erika.
Today there is no sign of brain damage or any other permanent
result of her terrible night in the cold. She laughs and plays
with other children, carrying no memory of her time in the
frigid valley of the shadow of death.

As I think of Erika, I think of John's words again:
Remember the height from which you have fallen! At one time,
you basked in the warm, safe, and secure presence of your
Father. But with the ignorance of a child, you strayed from His
warm, loving arms and wandered farther and farther away. The
time came when you found yourself out in the cold. You need
to be in God's arms again; you need to know His love and
warmth. But all you feel is coldness and confusion.

MISTAKES

Over the years, we have worked hard to make our marriage the best it can be.

On many occasions I had to travel for extended periods, and Vonette could not accompany me. I had to work hard to maintain the intimacy we had cultivated. Distance and time could easily have become obstacles, but it was a matter of pri-orities for us to keep anything from damaging the closeness we desired.

God's Spirit is beckoning to you, drawing you to Himself.

There have also been times when I have been irritable or insensitive to my wife. Early in our relationship, as the president of our college/young adult group at the First Presbyterian Church, I was called to counsel someone experiencing a crisis that could have caused great heartache and even scandal to a famous Christian family—even worse, to the family of God. The situation arose suddenly, and I had no opportunity to tell Vonette where I was. I left her sitting for hours after church in a hot car with no clue as to my whereabouts. I could have gotten a message to her, of course, if I had stopped to be more considerate. When I finally returned, Vonette, needless to say, was less than pleased! She felt that if the shoe had been on the other foot, I would have been upset with her. And she was right.

We had to talk that one out. As a matter of fact, we took some time at that early juncture in our marriage to reassess our relationship and our priorities. I discovered that, in many ways, I needed to be more loving and considerate toward her feel-ings. I needed to make a habit of apologizing when I failed her, acknowledging my wrongs, and working to change my ways.

That is exactly what I did. Good things came out of that mis-understanding and, as a result, I grew a bit in maturity as a husband. Growth is painful! But we have both learned a lot over the years. By really working at it, we have been able to maintain and then *deepen* the love that first drew us together. (Just a simple suggestion to help ensure a happy marriage when problems arise: Always be quick to say, "I am sorry. I was wrong. Please forgive me. I love you.")

Turning Back Toward Home

He was still a young man, but you might not have guessed it at first glance. In the space of a few months, his youthful vigor had given way to the pallor of hunger and illness.

He had lived the high life, if only for a season. He had run through a small fortune in cash without looking back. As long as the money held out, there were plenty of women, plenty of parties, plenty of good times. But when the last coins had fallen from his wallet, he was not really surprised to see the "friends" fall away, too. Now he was alone.

As the young man considered the heights he had once held, he discovered that high living and high standards were two separate things. The wild times and parties were no more than a cruel mirage, but his family and his home now appeared to be a higher place in life than he had realized. Father had cared for all his needs, sparing no expense, but he had taken all that for granted! Fine clothes, servants, a full table—and now he had to scramble for table scraps. Now he was little more than a slave, unfit for the lowest level of servant in the house-hold of his youth. There was no doubt about it—high living had made him a low-life young man.

The thought of it now pierced his heart. He saw for the

first time the corruption inside him—the foolish rebellion that had caused him to demand his money and leave. How could he have inflicted so much pain on his father for the price of a sack of coins? His eyes flooded with tears. There he sat, muddy, slumped against a trash bin in the worst part of town, weeping uncontrollably. The other beggars thought he was intoxicated, but he was filled with only remorse and homesickness.

The young man stood up and turned around, facing home with eyes and soul. He would make the long journey somehow, in the hope that he would be taken in and allowed to tend the animals. It was the worst job he could think of, but it did not matter—anything to be home again, anything to see his father. But how would he be received? Had his father disowned him?

After a long journey, he was slowly approaching the old familiar place at sunset. Squinting his eyes to see the estate, he caught sight of a dim figure by the side of the road. It was just an outline, a thin silhouette, yet the body language was unmistakable. The figure strained forward, as if studying the intersection of the road and the horizon—in *his* direction. The figure rose tentatively, then broke into a sprint up the road. It was the awkward gait of an older man who had not moved so quickly in years.

It was then that the young man knew—his father would meet him more than halfway. His homesickness was nothing compared to the grief his father had experienced over his absence. Tonight there would be a party—*such* a party! Its light would cast out the darkness of his wickedness, and its joy would erase the emptiness of squandered opportunities.

The familiar tale of the Prodigal Son (from Luke 15:11–32) is one more story of returning to the love of God once it has been left. The young man wandered from his father; he fell from the nobility of his birthright. Then, in true Revelation 2 form, he considered the height from which he had fallen. He felt deep remorse and turned his face toward home.

So Near, Yet So Far

Perhaps you have heard the story of a traveler who was on a business trip. As he drove down the main boulevard, he realized he had no idea how to find the convention center for his meeting. Being a humble man, he pulled his car over to the side of the road, rolled down his window, and hailed an elderly man sitting at a bus stop. "Excuse me, sir," he said. "Can you tell me how much farther it is to the convention center?"

> *You may feel many thousands of miles away from God today, but He is as close as a whispered prayer.*

The old man smiled and said, "I certainly can. It depends on which route you want to take. In the direction you're heading, it's many thousands of miles. If you turn your car in the opposite direction, however, it's a block and a half."

So near, and yet so far! You may feel many thousands of miles away from God today, but He is as close as a whispered prayer. The Bible tells us that He never removes His eye from us and never sleeps. If you can no longer see Him, it may well be that you're simply facing the wrong way. Nobody likes to stop to ask for directions, but isn't it so much worse to be lost? God is so near—just a 180-degree turn away.

Sometimes it takes a good bit of resolve to make that turn. You become comfortable in your sin. Your lungs become accustomed to bad air. But pollution is deadly; another word for it is

---❖---

"TURN BACK TO ME AGAIN."

REVELATION 2:5B

5

Repentance: Removing the Obstacles

In the Bible, the word "repentance" means a complete turnaround—both inside and outside. This desire for change comes from the depth of your soul.

Repentance is a lot more than simply feeling guilty. It means moving beyond guilt to transformation. It means turning from going your own, independent, self-centered way to embracing God's will for your life. You put one foot in front of the other and go back the way you came. That is the only way back to God. As you make that journey, our Lord will light your path. He promised, "I am the light of the world. If you follow me, you won't be stumbling through the darkness, because you will have the light that leads to life" (John 8:12).

Still, though you know Christ, you struggle with sin. I believe this is the critical point, the defining moment in being restored to your first love. How many Christians come to the aching awareness of being self-exiled from our dear Father? Most of us. How many really, truly repent, redirect, and return? Far fewer, I'm afraid. This could well be the most important chapter in the book for you. I pray that God will take each word and illuminate it specifically for your life and circumstances.

A Breath of Fresh Air

You might be aware that this chapter's topic is particularly close to my heart. For many years I was troubled by the observation that even after receiving Christ, so many people live in various degrees of defeat. Why, I wondered, was there so little love among many believers? And particularly, why did I so often struggle with my own sins and shortcomings? There were occasions when I was inconsiderate and self-centered, even though I knew that the Spirit of God lived within me.

Through the ministry of Campus Crusade for Christ, we had given all of our energies to helping take the gospel to the world—sharing the message of God's love and forgiveness through our Lord Jesus Christ. We were having a great deal of success. But we knew there had to be more than the acceptance of Christ: How could we help new believers maintain their first love for Christ and mature in their faith, love, and fruitfulness for Him?

I came to understand that sin steals back into our lives, even though Jesus has completely conquered it. He has removed the deadly venom from the serpent, Satan. Though defeated at the cross, that snake is still capable of biting if we do not keep our distance. I have seen it so often in my life as well as in the lives of people I know and love. We know Christ but we struggle with sin. Paul spoke of the conflict between the flesh and the Spirit in Galatians 5:16–17 (NIV):

> So I say, live by the Spirit, and you will not gratify the
> desires of the sinful nature. For the sinful nature desires

what is contrary to the Spirit, and the Spirit what is contrary to the sinful nature. They are in conflict with each other, so that you do not do what you want.

Many years ago, while grappling with this truth, I experienced a moment of inspiration. God showed me a word picture of a simple concept that I call "Spiritual Breathing." He helped me to understand that God's loving presence is much like the air I breathe. This one concept has enriched my life like no other. I discovered a way for me to take my sins and lay them before God even as I struggled with them. And over the years, I've been told by many other believers that the practice of Spiritual Breathing has liberated them spiritually.

Spiritual Breathing will help you deal with sin. You cannot live—*truly* live—without it. Believe me, I understand this concept of Spiritual Breathing more clearly now than ever. Because of my pulmonary fibrosis, I use a tube to help my lungs take in pure oxygen almost twenty-four hours a day. Every breath is precious. But many years ago, when my physical breathing was taken for granted, I first grasped this concept: I need to watch what comes into my system.

You dwell in a very polluted world, and you breathe in many unhealthy things every day. Often, while watching television or listening to music, you breathe in foul things from the world's culture. Spending time around certain people who are poor influences, you take in polluted ideas. You need to "exhale" the pollution of sin, and "inhale" the goodness of God's forgiveness and grace.

When you sin by committing a deliberate act of disobedience, Spiritual Breathing restores the fullness of God's Holy Spirit in your life. It is an exercise in faith that enables you to continue to experience God's love and forgiveness in your life. Spiritual Breathing is simply exhaling the impure and inhaling the pure.

EXHALE

Confess your sin—name each sin, agree with God concerning your sin, and thank Him for His forgiveness of it, according to 1 John 1:9. Confession involves repentance—a change in attitude and action.

INHALE

Surrender the control of your life to Christ, and appropriate (receive) the fullness of the Holy Spirit by faith. Trust that He now directs and empowers you according to the *command* of Ephesians 5:18 and the *promise* of 1 John 5:14–15.

Ever since the day this idea came so clearly to me, our ministry has taught the concept of Spiritual Breathing for daily, immediate confession of sin and for appropriating the fullness of the Holy Spirit by faith as a way of life. Your spiritual lungs are choking on foul air, and you do not even realize it. You must remember the height from which you've fallen—up on that spiritual mountaintop, where the air is pure and clean. Then you must take a deep breath of air administered by God's Spirit, and turn back toward the heights you would like to reach once more.

PRAYER AND FASTING

I would like to commend to you one further discipline. This one is seldom practiced but, like Spiritual Breathing, it will help you recapture your first love.

Over the last twenty-five years I have sensed the need for

spiritual revival in our country. The simple, personal principles that we are exploring in this book can also be applied to us as a nation. No one can dispute that our country has forsaken the first love it had for God two centuries ago. We as a nation need to remember the height from which we have fallen. We need to repent and return to the godliness and devotion that made our nation great in the past. The Bible teaches that just as an individual can consecrate him or herself to God, so an entire country can do the same on a corporate level. That is the reason millions of Americans are praying for revival.

To confront the deeper spiritual issues—the most stubborn strongholds of sin—we need to embark on a journey of intense prayer and fasting. Before revival can occur in this or any other nation, we need thousands, even millions, of believers fasting, praying, and seeking God's face. Prayer brings us directly into God's presence; fasting heightens our dependence and sensitivity to what He wants to say to us.

(Note: I recommend safe and healthy fasting, taking in liquids, vitamins, and minerals to meet your body's essential needs.)

Fasting and praying have certainly changed me. As I have dedicated myself to fast for forty days at a time each year since 1994, intensely seeking God's face, I have experienced many benefits, especially a greater intimacy with Him. I have experienced His leading with unprecedented clarity. I have written several books on this topic, and our ministry published an entire book of inspiring testimonies about fasting from across the nation. People have experienced personal repentance, spiritual revival, and a fresh vision from God through prayer and fasting. Many of them had previously been aware of the distance they had fallen from their first love for God. But somehow they lacked the true desire to change things in their lives—to exhale the impure influences that had taken hold of them. Through dedicated prayer and disciplined fasting, they were able to repent in a much more profound way.

I have many friends across America and the world who point to a forty-day fasting period as their defining moment—the watershed event in which they repented, turned their faces back to God, and once again experienced their first love.

In order to recapture your first love, you will certainly find it necessary to commit yourself more deeply to prayer. If the Holy Spirit reveals sins that have become obstructions in your life, and you find that you lack the motivation to change, you may find it necessary to seek the transforming presence of God through fasting. It will "jump-start" your process of repentance.

TURNAROUND LIST

In chapter 3, we talked about making a simple chart of your life now and comparing it with your life back when you were closer to God. I hope you've done that. Pray over the list. Ask God if there are any more items you need to add. Then I suggest you take a red pen and underline the ones that clearly identify sin in your life. The red ink might suggest the blood of Christ, which has already conquered each one of those items; they no longer hold any power to conquer you—not if you surrender them to Christ.

I trust you can identify at least three issues that call for repentance in your life. Probably there will be many more. Offer them to God. Use the eloquence of Psalms 32 and 51 to express to Him the sorrow in your heart. David wrote these moving words during his time of deepest failure. These psalms are the record of his profound sorrow, remorse, and journey back to the joy of God's presence. If God forgave him his terrible sins—adultery, murder, and deceit—is it not reasonable to believe that He will forgive and cleanse you?

With your "turnaround" list in hand, pray over each line of these psalms and apply these expressions of King David to your life. Believe me when I say that if you do this, you have reached the turning point in recovering your first love for God:

> Purify me from my sins, and I will be clean;
> wash me, and I will be whiter than snow.
> Oh, give me back my joy again;
> you have broken me—
> now let me rejoice.
>
> PSALM 51:7-8

> Oh, what joy for those
> whose rebellion is forgiven,
> whose sin is put out of sight!
> Yes, what joy for those
> whose record the LORD has cleared of sin,
> whose lives are lived in complete honesty!
> When I refused to confess my sin,
> I was weak and miserable,
> and I groaned all day long.
> Day and night your hand of discipline
> was heavy on me...
> Finally, I confessed all my sins to you
> and stopped trying to hide them.
> I said to myself, "I will confess my rebellion
> to the LORD." And you forgave me!

All my guilt is gone.
Therefore, let all the godly confess their
rebellion to you while there is time,
that they may not drown in the floodwaters of judgment.

PSALM 32:1–6

Repentance may involve a moment of pain. But no repentance ensures a *life* of pain. And beyond the moment of the about-face, the eternal joy of God's love is waiting. You have pursued God now with your mind, heart, and soul. One thing remains.

6

Resumption: Rejoining the Path of Obedience

When you see how far you have fallen, you are devastated by remorse—the mind engages the heart, and the heart engages the soul. It remains, as you will see, only for the hands to play their part. As the following story demonstrates, sorrow is worthwhile only if it leads to action. This is the third directive in Revelation 2:5: "Work as you did at first." In other words, *go back to the basics.* Resume.

Notice that Jesus does not say this to a lazy, inactive group of people. The first thing He mentioned was their vigorous activity. "I have seen your hard work and your patient endurance," He told them (Revelation 2:2). But their work had become empty. It had become like a loveless marriage, with all the routine but none of the romance.

SECOND CHANCE

In 1989, the University of Michigan played its conference rival Wisconsin in basketball. It was a close game, and Michigan trailed by a single point with only seconds remaining.

That was when Michigan's fine guard Rumeal Robinson stepped to the foul line for two shots.

It was the scenario every player dreams about. Robinson had the opportunity to be a hero; he had the game in his hands. If he simply hit one foul shot, he could tie the game and send it into overtime. If he put both shots through the net, his team would have an exciting win.

Robinson missed the first shot. Then he missed the second. Wisconsin's players ran off the course shouting with joy—they had upset the heavily favored Michigan Wolverines. And Rumeal Robinson, the All-American guard, was left standing at the line, hanging his head. He had failed, and in something so simple and fundamental.

Robinson felt great sorrow over that game. He had hit thousands of foul shots over the years, on his way to becoming one of the best shooting guards in college basketball. Growing up, he had stood under the hoop for hours until he could send shot after shot through the net, without even touching the rim. Why had he missed these two?

Some athletes never recover from the failure of a big game, but Robinson put his disappointment into action. He showed up at the next practice, played hard, then remained on the court afterward to shoot one hundred foul shots all by himself. For the rest of the season, that was his daily regimen—one hundred extra foul shots after every practice.

The day came, at the end of that season, when Rumeal Robinson found himself standing at the foul line again. This time there were three seconds remaining in overtime in the national championship game against Seton Hall. Both shots fell easily through the net. Michigan won the NCAA crown.

Today, few remember Robinson's two missed shots against

Wisconsin early in the season. But every Wolverine fan remembers the two graceful ones that brought home the championship. It all happened because Rumeal Robinson felt his failure deeply enough to return to the fundamentals—the things he did when he first loved basketball.

BACK TO THE BASICS

You may be serving God with energy and faithfulness—just like Martha was. What you may have failed to confront is the issue of first love because you are so busy doing all the right things. You go to church. You read your Bible. You offer a cup of cold water. Isn't that the same as love? Didn't Jesus identify love with obedience? The answer is yes. You *do* serve your Lord because you love Him—you have simply left the joy and the intimacy of Christ Himself. You have become so busy with your daily tasks that you have neglected to sit at His feet.

For example, in struggling marriages, both spouses tend to insist that they do still love each other. They continue to go through the motions and keep the marriage together. They do all the right things, even giving each other gifts at Christmas and birthdays. But what they've left behind is the joy and the intimacy. When that happens, service can no longer bring pleasure. Jesus wants you to see that. He would have you shift your focus from the lifeless things you're doing now to the loving things you did in the beginning. Always remember, living for Jesus is not only what you do for Him but, more importantly, what He does in and through you as you surrender yourself to Him in response to His love. "We love because he first loved us" (1 John 4:19 NIV).

That is why, at this point in your journey, it is important to "work as you did at first." When your heart has changed toward

God, and you have repented of the sin you discovered in your life, you are going to catch a second wind for serving Him. You will serve Him with new joy and dedication. You will go back to the basics.

Now, what are those basics?

THE SECOND TIME AROUND

The story is told of a man who was immersed in his newspaper one morning as he ate breakfast. Over the paper came the voice of his wife: "I bet you don't remember what today is."

Several alarms went off in the husband's head. "Of course I do, honey!" he said with a romantic kiss. Then he rushed out the door, hurried to his office, and picked up the telephone. Two-dozen roses were delivered to his wife—and right behind them, a gigantic box of candy. Finally, near the end of the day, a long limousine pulled up to the front door. The wife was speechless. Her husband helped her into the limousine with a big smile. On the way to the best restaurant in town, he said to his wife, "You see? I *do* remember the significance of today, don't I?"

"You certainly do," smiled his wife. "This has to be the most wonderful Groundhog Day I've ever spent!"

While that fellow may not have possessed the world's best sense of timing, he did understand something about getting back to the basics. He knew how to get to work in a relationship. I would assume that in the early days of their courting, this man did similar things—perhaps with a better feel for the occasion.

When you leave your first love, many things come between you and the Lord, just as surely as that fellow's newspaper was blocking the view. When you feel the deep sorrow of repentance and experience God's forgiveness and love, you want to do the things you once did. Some of these will be obvious—prayer and time in the Word, for example. Other activities for Him will take some thought and prompting by the Spirit.

When you first met Christ, you probably talked to Him frequently. How is your prayer life today? Has it become rigid and routine? Perhaps it would help to find a new place and a new approach for spending time with God. As mentioned earlier, it is a great idea to keep a prayer journal. Pour out your thoughts and your requests to God. Read the Psalms and record your personal responses to them. As God works in your life, write down your new thoughts and experiences. You will be able to return to these entries later and praise God anew, as more difficult events occur in your life. The more you know about someone, the more you have to talk about.

Take a fresh approach to your study of God's holy, inspired Word. Please do not think you can rediscover your first love for God without immersing yourself in His Book. That is the place where you feel the Spirit's touch most powerfully. That is where His great teachings for you are recorded. His truth will galvanize your life. Begin a new, exciting study of the Bible. Read it cover-to-cover. Or focus on the Gospels. Go to a Christian bookstore and look for a volume that will jump-start your devotional times.

Once again, think of the things you first did—the "flowers and candy" of your early times with God. How did you practice His presence in your daily life back then? How did you talk to others about Him? What were your relationships like? Review the chart you made earlier to help you get back to the basics.

My friends, a fresh new joy can drive your actions. But it

works the other way, too. If you have seen the "fact, faith, and feeling" train diagram in *The Joy of Finding Jesus* or other books in this series, you understand that feelings are simply the result of faith and obedience. In other words, do not wait to feel something in order to do something. Know that you can *act* your way into *feeling* much more effectively than you can feel your way into acting. Go share your faith in Christ with someone, whether you feel like it or not. Simply breathe spiritually and ask God to lead you to someone who needs Him. Serve God in a new way. Go downtown and volunteer for a mission project for the poor, and see if that does not energize your love for God. Spend time teaching children or teenagers at your church about our Lord. Encourage a struggling friend. I guarantee you, the feelings will come naturally from your attention to the things God cares about. Ask God to break your heart with the things that grieve Him.

Also, do things that will require you to walk in faith. You may lose the feeling for God's Spirit because you are not doing anything in life that absolutely requires His presence and power. I challenge you to "put God on the spot" today. After you have confessed all known sin and have the assurance that you are filled with the Holy Spirit, ask Him to lead you to one nonbeliever who needs to hear the good news of Jesus Christ. Ask Him to put you right in the middle of a situation in which you can be His agent. See how real He will become in your life as you depend on Him to do something supernatural.

When you leave something behind, you retrace your steps back to the place where you left it. Return to the basics—I predict you will find your Lord there, right where you left Him. He is waiting for you.

LOVING BY FAITH

One of the greatest lessons I have learned in my marvelous adventure with Christ is *how to love by faith*. And I learned that life-changing truth during one of the most difficult periods of my life.

One early morning in 1967, a group of thirteen of my beloved fellow staff, whom I had discipled and to whom I had delegated great responsibilities, confronted me with an ultimatum. I was to resign the presidency of Campus Crusade for Christ, which Vonette and I had founded in 1951, or they would take over the movement. They declared that the entire staff of several hundred would follow their leadership.

After they gave me the ultimatum, that very night God awakened me at 2 a.m. with a message. I had learned to walk closely with our Lord and always sought to listen carefully to any impression I may receive from Him. I tried to live according to the promise of Philippians 2:13: "It is God who works in you to will and to act according to his good purpose" (NIV). In other words, whatever God tells you to do, He will give you the power to do if you love, trust, and obey Him.

In obedience to His leading, I got out of bed, took my Bible, and went into another room. I knelt before God with the prayer, "Lord, do you have something to say to me?" For the next two hours, He showed me not only the importance of loving those who had rejected my leadership, but also *how* to love them.

Though His message from His Word was far more detailed, the distilled essence of what God said to me was very simple. It involved two very important words: *command* and *promise*. I am commanded to love God with all of my mind, heart, soul, and strength, and to love my neighbors as myself (Luke 10:27). I am commanded to love my fellow believers (John 13:34–35) and even my enemies (Matthew 5:44).

I know that it is His will that I love Him and others because that is His *command*. So, by faith, I asked God to help me love others according to His *promise* in 1 John 5:14–15 (NIV):

> This is the confidence we have in approaching God: that if we ask anything according to his will, he hears us. And if we know that he hears us—whatever we ask—we know that we have what we asked of him.

That night, I determined, with God's help, to love each of these men who had been unfaithful to my trust, whatever happened. As a result, I continued to love them then, and still do to this day. God never allowed me to defend myself. In fact, He fought for me. While only six of these key men ultimately left the ministry, the Lord of the harvest sent over seven hundred new full-time staff to join us that very summer.

Some months later the leader of the coup returned to ask my forgiveness. He explained that the phenomenal success they were experiencing across the country had led them to think more highly of themselves than they had reason to think. "We were on an ego trip," he confessed. "We were wrong. Please forgive us."

You love others in the same way you love God. You obey His *command* to love Him and others, and you claim His *promise* that if you ask anything according to His will, He will hear and answer. By faith based on His command and promise, you can love God with all your heart, soul, mind, and strength.

7

Revival: Rejoicing in the Light

The most striking element of the story of the prodigal son, in my opinion, is not its depiction of the son's sorrow. The greatest truth is seen in its dazzling portrait of our Father's forgiveness. He waits patiently for the son to return and greets him with precisely the opposite of the reaction we might expect.

While the son was still a long distance away, his father saw him coming. Filled with love and compassion, he ran to his son, embraced him, and kissed him (Luke 15:20). With this father there is no bitterness or recrimination. He has absolutely no thought of demanding that the son earn his way back into his graces, as the son is more than ready to do.

The compassion of this father is deeply moving. This message says everything you need to know about the loving heart of our Lord because, my friend, only the details are different from those of your life. That's how Jesus welcomes us home.

Is your image of God consistent with the portrait in Luke 15? Jesus wants us to see that God is like this father who is wildly joyful, overflowing with love and compassion, embracing and kissing a son who surely smells of filthy hogs, a dusty journey, and a sordid life. Neither the rags, the smell, nor the wrongs of the past mean anything at all to this father—only the heart that turned toward home. God is just like that.

Oh, if only you could indelibly etch such a picture of God into your heart and mind! How much easier would it be to maintain your first love? And how it would overwrite all those messages of defeat and failure that consume the way you live.

I think too many of us have the opposite idea of God. Do you imagine Him glowering at you behind the fortress walls of heaven, scowling as you pound on the door. You know you've sinned, and you're afraid of the inevitable confrontation with His anger and derision. You imagine Him sitting within those walls smoldering with wrath, measuring out eternity in punishments to answer your rebellion. If that is your understanding, it is tragically inaccurate—and no wonder you are afraid to turn *or* return to Him.

Yes, God does hate the cheap sins and false gods for which we desert Him. He *does* have wrath, and He does judge sin. But He looks upon His stray children with love and compassion. He waits with His eyes on the horizon, day after day. Then—before you can even return to Him—He meets you halfway, heaping blessings upon blessings on your head, declaring a celebration in heaven. Remember the father in Luke 15. He killed the finest calf, the best he had, the one he was saving for the ultimate celebration.

The moment you take one sorrowful, halting step in the Father's direction, His joy overflows. He bestows the deepest blessings, the good things He has been storing away for you. His joy cannot be contained. It has been said that when you take one step toward God, He takes more steps toward you than there are sands on the beaches of the world.

Earlier in Luke 15, Jesus describes how God comes after you. He tells the story of a shepherd who leaves his great flock of sheep to find the lost one. Jesus says in closing the story: "There will be more rejoicing in heaven over one sinner who repents than over ninety-nine righteous persons who do not need to repent" (v. 7 NIV).

What I want most for you to see in this chapter is the overwhelming joy of God over your return to your first love. When you have been reunited with the Good Shepherd, your joy cannot even compare to the boundless delight He feels.

God will rejoice over you as a bridegroom rejoices over his bride (Isaiah 62:5).

Isn't that a wonderful thing to know?

LIFE IN THE LIGHT

When you repent and return to your first love, you will experience the joy you long for—a revival of your spirit. In David's moving prayer of repentance, he prayed:

> Create in me a pure heart, O God, and renew a steadfast
> spirit within me...Restore to me the joy of your salvation
> and grant me a willing spirit, to sustain me.
>
> PSALM 51:10, 12 NIV

How will your life change when you've rediscovered your first love? I believe there are three changes that will take place in your life.

First, your intimacy with God will grow to become deeper, more profound, and more rewarding. Some of those unworthy ideas about God—that He is always frowning, shaking His head and grumbling as He looks at you, for instance—will fade away in the light of His genuine nature. You will bask in the true warmth of His love, grace, and compassion. So transforming, so gratifying will that experience be that you will not be able to leave His side after you return to your first love. Instead, you will practice His presence wherever you go. Yes, you will abide in prayer for richer, more generous portions of your day not because you have to, but because you want to. You'll also develop a renewed desire to spend time in God's Word. And you'll take that sweet time of fellowship with Him wherever you go all during the day. His presence will become a way of life.

His presence will become a way of life.

As a result, you will see your life and experiences through new eyes. You will avoid poor decisions and temptations that might have tripped you up in the past. You will abide with Christ, and He will abide with you. And as this happens, He will be slowly sculpting you into His image. In time, you will be an entirely new person—one who bears a greater resemblance to your Lord, and one who bears a lesser resemblance to the old self who lived selfishly and in rebellion. And wonderful fruit will spring up in your life, for your ministry in the world will be greatly enhanced.

Expect a life lived in God's love that will make a difference in the lives of others. You will begin to have a significant impact on other people. Your relationships will be far more dynamic than they have ever been. John wrote, "If we are living in the light of God's presence, just as Christ is, then we have fellowship with each other, and the blood of Jesus, his Son, cleanses us from every sin" (1 John 1:7). That first chapter was one of the first I memorized when I became a believer in Christ. These truths had a powerful impact on my life. I realized that loving God leads to loving people, because Christ died for them. That is why Vonette and I responded to Christ's call to help fulfill His Great Commission in our generation.

You will have a greater compassion toward others, and others will be more attracted to you as well. A friend once asked Charles Wesley why people were drawn magnetically to him everywhere he went. Wesley replied, "When you set your-self on fire, people just love to come and watch you burn." Those around you will see the spiritual fire, the "first love," within you, and they will be motivated and inspired by your example. You will not be able to resist sharing the fire—but even if you did not say a word,

I realized that loving God leads to loving people, because Christ died for them.

you would find yourself drawn into conversations about Jesus. A city on a hill cannot be hidden. You will stand out in your world, and people will have questions about the burning passion in your eyes and your work. Your greatest joy in life will come from helping other people to find the same joy you have found in knowing, loving, trusting, and obeying our dear Lord.

If you are married, your marital relationship, too, will be enhanced by your first love for God. You will learn how to love your spouse sacrificially as Christ loves His bride. If you are a parent, you will care for your family flock in a way that reflects the wisdom of the Good Shepherd. If you have a career, you will relate to your coworkers in a way that sets you apart as His workmanship. As you abide in the presence and love of God, your relationships will never be the same again.

The third change in your life will be that God's love will flood your heart with His peace. The world is filled with people in turmoil. Every single person was made to live and thrive on the love of our wonderful God. When you try to live in any other way, you can only find yourself eventually at war within. You become like the prodigal, picking at scraps in the trash bins of the world when you could be dining at the table of our King. You sense there is more, and you know there must be abundant living somehow. Whether you seek peace through money, fame, possessions, pleasure, or some other cheap substitute, you will find no lasting happiness until the love of God envelops you with His supernatural peace.

————————◆————————

We are not fighting a civil war within our souls. Our first love has helped us to maintain our inner peace.

Vonette and I do not think of our contract to be slaves of Jesus as a sacrifice—anything but! It is the most liberating action we could ever have taken. Because of our love and our deep gratitude for all He has done for us, we chose to surrender ourselves and all that we possessed or ever would possess to Him, our great God and Savior. As a result we have been spared many worries and anxieties. We have not pursued fame or glory, wealth, praise, or applause of others, but instead we have offered ourselves as His slaves for His glory. We signed our commitment as a fully binding contract and we have approached it seriously, like any other contract, ever since. We have therefore been freed from pettiness, resentment, and competitive internal and external conflicts. We have the freedom and energy to do the things God has called us to do, because we are not fighting a civil war within our souls. Our first love has helped us to maintain our inner peace.

Have you found a peace such as this? Are you experiencing the sweet presence of God every day, everywhere you go under all circumstances? Are you a transforming influence among the people who surround you, rather than conforming to their pattern? The love of God will set you free. It will enable you to experience the abundant life that Jesus promised to all who love, trust, and obey Him.

TURNING HOMEWARD

Friend, the God you seek is Someone who seeks you even more intensely. To experience the full and complete joy of reunion with Him, you need only to have responded in faith and obedience to the suggestions we have discussed in this book:

With your mind, you have remembered the height from which you have fallen. You have reflected deeply upon the joy of God's presence and the pain of being apart from Him.

With your heart, you have experienced remorse over the place where your wandering has brought you. When you truly comprehend the despair and judgment that await us without God, it is natural to feel grief and sorrow.

From your soul, you have repented of the sin that ensnared you and stifled your first love. You have genuinely, sincerely renounced the things that have come between you and God.

With your strength, enabled by the Holy Spirit, you have resumed the things you once did to please God. Just as the Prodigal traveled home, you have emotionally and spiritually turned toward your heavenly home as you have returned to your first love for your great God and Savior.

With your total being, you are now revived; you have returned to your "first love." Your mind, heart, soul, and strength have been renewed. You are now experiencing again the joy of your salvation, which you may not have known for years. Now you love God with every fiber of your being.

As you have embraced the above action, you are already feeling the deep joy of your reunion with God. The party has begun! Now take special time to worship and praise your God, even as He celebrates your return. Consider a full day or more to retreat to a place where you can pray, sing, worship, and reflect upon the goodness of God—and allow His refreshing love to sink into your soul. And do not forget to keep serving Him with your hands.

One way you might do that is to tell a friend about the deep, incredible joy you are experiencing. Only one thing would thrill your Father's heart more than the sight of you approaching home after your prodigal journey. That would be the sight of *two* figures: you and a friend whom you have invited to share your first love for our dear Savior.

And though you're prone to wander, make it your daily prayer that you'll never leave your first love. When you remain true to your first love, you'll be on a lifetime adventure of joy and peace.

8

Reward: Resting in the Shade of Eternity

I magine slowly awakening, as if from a wonderful, refreshing sleep. It feels as if you're a child again, waking to the first morning of a glorious spring. You are filled with the kind of youthful energy and excitement you have not felt in—well, far too long.

You yawn, stretch, and feel the gentleness of the breeze rippling your hair. The dampness of the dew is beneath your bare feet. It is clear that you are outdoors, though you cannot quite remember why. And the last dream of your slumber seems just beyond your grasp. Where are you?

There is a stone wall that is hard to ignore. It rises sturdily behind you and encircles you. It appears that you are enclosed in a lush, circular garden. Just beyond your feet are flowers—flowers such as you've never seen before, exploding with the color of light at the height of their bloom. They rise gracefully to the crest of a hill at the very center of the garden. And there at the crest, towering majestically into the sky, is an amazing tree.

From the moment that tree fills your eyes, you can look

upon nothing else. Surely there is no other tree like it on earth—if indeed earth holds this dreamland in which you've found yourself. The great, colossal trunk must be many thousands of years old. The roots must sink to the very core of the world. And the branches must reach somewhere beyond the sky. There are so many of those branches entwining themselves into the clouds that you cannot count them.

Then you see it—the one fruit, hanging from its vine and dancing softly in the breeze.

What kind of fruit is it? It is not an apple—not exactly. It is not a peach or pear. Nor is it any member of the citrus family. It is not a fruit like any you have seen before. Yet somehow you know that it is there for *you*. It has been waiting there, ever ripe, ever sweet, since the day you were born. No doubt, the purpose of your life has been to come to this place and taste this delicious fruit.

Closing your eyes, you taste it eagerly—and suddenly your eyes open to a new world.

This story is a simple retelling of Revelation 2:7, the encouragement Jesus offers to the church at Ephesus: "Everyone who is victorious will eat from the tree of life in the paradise of God."

If you know your Bible well, you have caught the beautiful symmetry of that passage found on the final pages of the Scriptures. In Genesis, Adam and Eve were placed in a perfect garden. They were able to walk and talk with God, enjoying the deepest fellowship with Him. But one action was forbidden to them: They were not to eat from a certain tree. As we all know, they did it anyway—and they left their first love, their first home, and their first access to God. They left behind their immortality, too. Concerned that Adam and Eve would then eat from the tree of life and remain forever in their spiritual state—separated from God—He evicted them from the garden.

But in Revelation 2 we find the wonderful conclusion to the story. It says, "To him who overcomes, I will give to eat from the tree of life, which is in the midst of the Paradise of God" (NKJV). It turns out that some will eat from that tree of life even yet—with God's full blessing. And they will have full, perfect, and unbroken fellowship with God forever, in a way that even Adam and Eve, in their initial perfection, never experienced. The original Greek language uses, for *paradise*, a word of Persian origin meaning "a garden surrounded by a wall."

> *That love, you see, is your hope. It is your foretaste of glory divine.*

How has the wall come to surround the first home of Adam and Eve? It was placed there by sin—theirs and ours. And how are we described in verse 7? As people who are "victorious." Other translations describe us as those who "overcome" or "conquer." Jesus is speaking to those who walk through walls.

And how do you do that? Through the Lord Jesus Christ—the Overcomer, the Conqueror, the Victor. Jesus has finally brought you back to that garden where it all began. And this is the ultimate conclusion of first love—that you recover the perfect relationship with God that mankind left at the beginning of time. You will finally spend your days face to face with the King who planted the garden and set the tree in place, who has waited for all time until the day when you would remain with Him forever.

My word skills are limited, but I hope you can appreciate the breathtaking beauty of this scene. You may not taste the delicious juices of that fruit for a little while, but for now you cling to your first love. That love, you see, is your hope. It is your *foretaste* of glory divine. As you taste the love of God, you bloom spiritually in a way that is no less majestic than that tree. Your roots are set in eternity. You lift your hands to the heavens, worshiping the One who tends and waters us. And you produce wonderful fruit in its season.

Without the love of God, of course, life is not majestic at all. Life is dry, empty. Your branches produce only dead leaves. The very roots are decayed, and you can sense the dust of death. Life without God's love is nothing more than despair and longing. It is not a life worth living.

I think back now over half a century, since 1945, when I was first awakened to the wonder of His love for me. It seemed then, and seems now, a miracle. I cannot quite think of myself as a tree—it is easier for me to imagine myself as an insignificant little termite somewhere gnawing on the roots. And yet I know that God sees in me the potential He created me to attain one day. He loves me. I know that I've loved Him more fully with each passing year. I know that I am only able to properly love Vonette, our children and grandchildren, our many friends, our brothers and sisters in Christ, and the entire world because He lives within me and loves them through me.

My Lord has blessed me with so much abundance, so much love, so many thrilling plans worth pursuing, that I find it impossible at eighty to adapt to retirement and to "slow down." I love the life He has given me in this world. And yet I know that the day will come when I will awake without the oxygen tubes on which I now depend. I will feel full strength and vigor in these legs again. I will have the ability to run like the wind. But my only desire, upon awakening, will be to taste of the fruit of the tree of life—to know that I have all of eternity to learn about my Savior and discover God's glorious attributes. "All that I know now is partial and incomplete, but then I will know everything completely, just as God knows me now" (1 Corinthians 13:12).

If this love I have now—this first love—is only partial, I have to say that I long for the final edition. If the abundance of this life is only a foretaste, I long for the full meal. And if my comprehension of God now is just a glance through a hazy mirror, I long for a complete and unimpaired view. Praise God, what a day that will be! I can hardly wait. But for now, I have something wonderful. It cannot compare to the glories of heaven, but it is still the most wonderful thing in this world. I refer to the indescribable love of God.

Cling to that hope. Cherish it and nurture it every day. Make your first love be your lasting, permanent love, and God will grant you wonderful blessings beyond any imagining. And be sure to share your renewed first love with others.

If you sincerely desire to return to your first love for God, please pray this prayer now and regularly for the rest of your life.

> Father in heaven, I sincerely desire to love You with all of my mind, heart, soul, and strength. And I want to love my family, my neighbors and friends, even my enemies. I realize that I am incapable of loving You and others in my own strength. So, on the authority of Your command to love and Your promise to hear and answer this prayer, I claim by faith that in the mighty name of Jesus You will answer my prayer.

PART TWO

Maintaining an Intimate Relationship with God

———◆———

"LOVE THE LORD YOUR GOD WITH ALL YOUR HEART AND
WITH ALL YOUR SOUL AND WITH ALL YOUR MIND."

MATTHEW 22:37 NIV

9

An Invitation to Intimacy with God

Imagine you have just received an invitation in the mail. As you open the envelope you discover it is from a celebrity known as the most powerful and honorable person in the world. For some inexplicable reason, this famous person wants to be your friend. But you must indicate your desire to pursue the relationship. How will you respond?

You may be thinking, *Nobody that important would ever choose me as a friend.* But someone already has! Your invitation did not come by mail; it was delivered in the Bible. The invitation was not only printed with ink, but was written with the blood of the sender. It does not come from merely a world-class celebrity, but from our all-powerful Creator God and Savior.

DEVELOPING INTIMACY WITH GOD

God is the one who spoke more than one hundred billion galaxies into existence. It is He who gave us life and sustains it with every breath we take (Job 33:4; Acts 17:25). He is the supreme Sovereign of the universe before whom all must bow (Romans 14:11). His abilities are infinite and His character is flawless.

From creation, your magnificent God has actively sought a love relationship with every person on earth. He created you in His image and longs for you to have intimate fellowship with Him. But how is it possible to experience such a wholehearted love relationship with God?

God has taken the initiative to establish a relationship with you. Because it is impossible for sinful creatures to have fellowship with a holy God, He came to earth in the person of His only begotten Son, Jesus of Nazareth, to die on the cross for all your sins.

This awesome truth is illustrated by the experience of a Hindu who was seeking God. When he heard about how Jesus came to live on this earth, he could not understand why the great God and Creator of the universe would want to humble Himself in that way.

God does not need your love or devotion.

Because of his religious background, he had a reverence for all forms of life. One day as he was walking in a field, he noticed a large anthill. He stopped to observe the activity of these amazing creatures.

Suddenly, he heard the noise of a tractor plowing the field. The plow would soon destroy that anthill! The ants' home would be gone and thousands killed. He was frantic! He thought, *How can I forewarn them? How can I save them from impending death? I could write a warning in the dirt, but they wouldn't know how to read it. I could shout to them, but they wouldn't recognize my voice. The only possible way I could communicate with them would be to become an ant myself.*

Then he understood why our loving God, the Sovereign of

the universe, had made such an incredible sacrifice to become one of us. The God-Man, Jesus of Nazareth, died on a cross to save humans from getting plowed under by sin.

But each person must individually accept God's forgiveness for sins by receiving His Son, Jesus Christ, as Lord and Savior (Romans 10:9). When you do this, you become one of God's adopted children (John 1:12–13) and acceptable to Him because Jesus clothes you with His righteousness (Isaiah 61:10; 2 Corinthians 5:2).

Through Jesus, God has made Himself knowable to you as explained in the Bible (John 1:1, 14; 14:9; 1 John 1:1–2; 5:20).

In addition, God indwells believers through His Holy Spirit (1 John 4:13; Galatians 4:6). Jesus told His disciples:

> I will ask the Father, and he will give you another
> Counselor, who will never leave you. He is the Holy Spirit,
> who leads into all truth. The world at large cannot receive
> him, because it isn't looking for him and doesn't recognize
> him. But you do, because he lives with you now and later
> will be in you.
>
> JOHN 14:16–17

Everything in your Christian life depends on the Holy Spirit living in you. Paul testifies, "We know how dearly God loves us, because he has given us the Holy Spirit to fill our hearts with his love" (Romans 5:5). The Spirit is the source of your new birth (John 6:63). He is your teacher and guide (1 Corinthians 2:10). He enables you to pray effectively (Romans 8:26–27) and comforts you in adversity. He empowers you to be a witness for Jesus. He produces the fruit of the Spirit in your life.

God does not need your love or devotion. He is completely self-sufficient and has no needs. Although the contrast is infinitely greater, it would be like you demonstrating loving concern to an ant. That ant can do nothing in return to warrant your attention.

Yet God wants you to fully experience and respond to His love and grace because He wants to bless and enrich your life. He promises, "If you look for me in earnest, you will find me when you seek me" (Jeremiah 29:13). Since this is true, why do so few of us have a dynamic relationship with our Creator, God, and Savior?

Seeking God wholeheartedly means making Him the focus of your love, desire, and entire being. When you seek God with your whole heart, your desire for closeness and intimacy with Him becomes increasingly consuming. He becomes the center of your life. All other relationships and activities are enriched by His love for you and your love for Him.

But you may be thinking, *I would like to seek God, but how can I develop and maintain a relationship with someone I can't see?*

A child and parent, husband and wife, or two friends need to spend time together and practice healthy interaction to have a loving relationship. I find many similarities between my relationship with Vonette, my wife, and the love relationship I have with God, my Savior. The same principles that help develop healthy human relationships help develop intimacy with the heavenly Father. Let us examine seven ways to strengthen our relationship with Him.

10

Desire Intimacy with God

Imagine for a moment being head-over-heels in love with someone who is not interested in you. You would feel hurt and disappointed. How could somebody possibly reject your genuine love? The driving force in every relationship is desire. Without mutual desire you cannot have a healthy relationship—only disappointment.

Imagine how God must feel when you do not respond to His love and offer of intimacy. Compared to Him, humans are less than microscopic parasites. You exist because of His provision. Everything you enjoy is a gift of His grace. Even the air you breathe and the water you drink are tokens of His love. At the cross He made the greatest possible sacrifice on your behalf. What arrogance and foolishness humans display when we ignore or neglect our relationship with God!

Before Vonette and I married, we were engaged for three years as she finished college. She was attending the prestigious Women's University in Denton, Texas, while I owned my own business and lived in Hollywood. During that time, we corresponded regularly through letters, telephone calls, and gifts—and I visited her as often as I could.

I worked at building my relationship with Vonette. And since our marriage on December 30, 1948, as I continue learning more about my wonderful wife, I grow to love her more deeply each day.

In like manner, I have invested considerable desire and effort to know God. The time I spend with my Savior is invaluable, and the more I know of Him, the more I love Him and want to do what pleases Him.

How strong is your desire for a more intimate relationship with Him? Building a relationship with God takes time and effort—but there is no investment that yields a better return. Your loving Creator longs for you to know Him.

King David's intimate love relationship with God is a model. Consider his advice to Solomon, "My son, get to know the God of your ancestors. Worship and serve him with your whole heart and with a willing mind ... If you seek him, you will find him" (1 Chronicles 28:9).

Compared to God, humans are less than microscopic parasites.

God is pursuing you and He wants you to pursue Him. The greatest of the commandments is to "love the Lord your God with all your heart, all your soul, and all your mind" (Matthew 22:37). Your Lord initiated the relationship and cleared away the obstacles through unimaginable sacrifice. Your loving Savior graciously continues to reach out to you with nail-scarred hands. However, your relationship with Him depends on your response (John 14:23).

King David writes, "O God ... I earnestly search for you. My soul thirsts for you; my whole body longs for you in this parched and weary land where there is no water ... Your unfailing love is better to me than life itself" (Psalm 63:1, 3). Without life-sustaining water, you would die. Do you long for God as much as you desire food and water, and even life itself?

Ask God to create in you an increasing desire for Him. Although desire is an emotion, it can be directed by your will. Choose to desire God. Do tangible things that move you closer to Him. Schedule time alone with Him to read the Scriptures, pray, and worship Him. With the Holy Spirit's help, you will feel new love and desire for your wonderful God and Savior.

"THOSE WHO OBEY MY COMMANDMENTS ARE THE ONES WHO LOVE ME. AND BECAUSE THEY LOVE ME, MY FATHER WILL LOVE THEM, AND I WILL LOVE THEM. AND I WILL REVEAL MYSELF TO EACH ONE OF THEM."

—JESUS CHRIST

11

Respect God and His Rules

Has a friend or loved one ever betrayed your trust? Their actions hurt the relationship. Everyone has values that must be respected or the friendship suffers. These problems must be resolved before the friendship can grow.

Fortunately, Vonette and I have had very few major disagreements during our fifty-one marvelous years of marriage. But I remember one time when I made a significant decision affecting her responsibilities without seeking her counsel. Vonette was so upset with me that she got in the car with our two young sons and started to drive away. I knew that I needed to make things right so I stepped in front of the car and blocked her departure. I apologized for my insensitivity and asked for her forgiveness. After a heartfelt discussion, our close relationship was restored.

That is similar to your relationship with God. But He does not turn away when you sin. He is always ready to forgive you. Whenever you disobey, you are the one who turns your back on Him.

As we read on a previous page, Jesus explained that your obedience to His commandments indicates your love for Him. He told His disciples, "I do nothing without consulting the Father" (John 5:30). That is the attitude He wants you to have toward Him as well. Isaiah proclaimed, "LORD, we love to obey your laws; our heart's desire is to glorify your name. All night long I search for you; earnestly I seek for God" (Isaiah 26:8–9).

Your obedience demonstrates respect (reverential fear) for God, who is worthy of highest honor. The Bible promises, "Friendship with God is reserved for those who reverence Him. With them alone He shares the secrets of His promises" (Psalm 25:14 TLB).

Reverential fear of God will keep you from sin.

When I come into the presence of my Sovereign God and the Ruler of the universe, I recognize that He deserves more reverence and respect than I show to any human. God is not the "man upstairs." He is my holy, righteous, omnipotent, awesome Creator and Savior. I must never be flippant or too casual with God.

Psalm 147:11 explains, "The LORD delights in those who fear him, who put their hope in his unfailing love" (NIV). I must approach my heavenly Father with humility, submissiveness, and a sense of wonder, because He can accomplish more than I can imagine.

Fearing God helps me to obey Him more consistently. I would rather God take my life before I engage in anything that would dishonor Him—whether it would be unfaithfulness to Vonette, stealing, or causing a scandal.

I live daily in reverential fear of God because I know that if

I disobey Him, I open the door to Satan for greater temptations. Major sin always starts with smaller sins. Unconfessed sin grows until it engulfs us in destruction. King David understood that sin also obstructs communication with God. He testifies, "If I had not confessed the sin in my heart, my Lord would not have listened" (Psalm 66:18).

Reverential fear of God will keep you from sin. But if you break His rules, God will discipline you because He loves you (Hebrews 12:5–11).

How is your relationship with your heavenly Father? Are you trying to stay pure for God? Is there unconfessed sin interrupting your fellowship with Him? If so, tell Him about it now. He promises, "If we confess our sins to him, he is faithful and just to forgive us and to cleanse us from every wrong" (1 John 1:9).

---❖---

I PRAY FOR YOU CONSTANTLY, ASKING GOD ... TO GIVE YOU
SPIRITUAL WISDOM AND UNDERSTANDING, SO THAT YOU
MIGHT GROW IN YOUR KNOWLEDGE OF GOD.

EPHESIANS 1:16–17

12

Understand God Better

S uppose your grandfather recently passed away. As you sort through his things, you find a notebook containing an autobiography that he wrote to share with his family. He wanted his descendants to have a record of the major events, significant relationships, and philosophical beliefs that shaped his life—and in turn helped to shape theirs. Would you put it back on the shelf, give it to other relatives, or take time to read it to know more about him?

God inspired holy men of old to record His "autobiography." Called the Holy Bible, its pages reveal liberating truths and life-changing insights. The priority you place on reading, studying, and memorizing Scripture indicates the importance you place on knowing Him.

Knowledge is the foundation for a relationship. When Vonette and I were separated by fifteen hundred miles for much of our engagement, we cherished the telephone calls and letters received from each other almost daily. They were vital to the development of our relationship.

You must have a right understanding of God because your

view of Him determines your lifestyle. What you believe to be true about God's character affects your relationships, work and leisure, the friends you choose, the type of literature you read, and even the music you enjoy. Everything about your life—your attitudes, motives, desires, actions, and even your words—is influenced by your view of God.

> *You must have a right understanding of God because your view of Him determines your lifestyle.*

The Bible contains God's love letters to you. These are the words of our Creator, the heavenly Father who adopted you, the loving Savior who died for you, the Holy Spirit who indwells you.

The Bible has been supernaturally infused with power to accomplish the eternal objectives of its divine Author. Jesus says, "The very words I have spoken to you are spirit and life" (John 6:63). The author of Hebrews explains, "The word of God is full of living power. It is sharper than the sharpest knife, cutting deep into our innermost thoughts and desires. It exposes us for what we really are" (Hebrews 4:12).

God's Word is a lamp to illuminate your life's journey (Psalm 119:105). It is a sword with which to battle temptation and deception (Ephesians 6:17). It is a seed that grows in fertile hearts to produce abundant faith and righteousness (Luke 8:11, 15). And it is a living letter that reveals the heart of your loving God and Savior.

The supreme purpose for humans is to know their God and Savior. Paul writes, "Everything else is worthless when compared with the priceless gain of knowing Christ Jesus my Lord. I have discarded everything else, counting it all as garbage, so that I may have Christ" (Philippians 3:8). Jesus wants to live

His life in and through you (Galatians 2:20). But you must get to know Him better.

Use the following questions to stimulate new interest in reading God's Word:

- God's attributes: What are God's character traits?
- God's names: How do God's names reflect His roles in relating to His people?
- God's purposes: What are God's plans and priorities?
- God's ways: What are God's methods?
- God's blessings: How has God demonstrated His love for you?
- God's commandments: What does God want you to do?
- God's promises: How has God committed Himself to you?
- God's resources: How does God empower you, help you, and provide for you?

As I read the Scriptures, I ask the Holy Spirit: "Open my spiritual eyes so I will see Your truth; enlighten my mind so I will understand what You are saying; soften my heart so I will obediently apply Your Word."

Your daily Bible reading will take on a new vibrancy when you read God's Word to know Him better.

I KNOW THE LORD IS ALWAYS WITH ME. I WILL NOT BE
SHAKEN, FOR HE IS RIGHT BESIDE ME.

PSALM 16:8

13

Enjoy God's Presence

When you love someone, you enjoy being with that person. To build a relationship, two people have to spend time together. Because of ministry and other responsibilities, my wife and I are away from home much of the time, but whenever possible we travel together. Even when we are at home and I am working on a special project by myself, it makes me feel so good to know my beloved Vonette is with me.

When you invited Christ into your life, the Holy Spirit came to reside in your heart. Paul explains, "We are the temple of the living God. As God said: 'I will live in them and walk among them. I will be their God, and they will be My people'" (2 Corinthians 6:16). Meditate on this marvelous promise from God's Word. You have the presence of the almighty God living inside you. Your body is His temple (1 Corinthians 3:16)!

Throughout the day as I talk to Him, the Lord Jesus speaks to me through His Word and through impressions in my mind. No matter what I am doing, it is so wonderful to know that He is with me. In difficult situations He reminds me, "I am holding you by your right hand—I, the LORD your God. And I say to you, 'Do not be afraid. I am here to help you'" (Isaiah 41:13). When the pressures are great and the problems are overwhelming, I thank my faithful Lord and Savior for His never-ending commitment: "Be strong and courageous! Do not be afraid of them! The LORD your God will go ahead of you. He will neither fail you nor forsake you" (Deuteronomy 31:6).

Unfortunately, you may go through the day ignoring His presence. You may waste so many opportunities for fellowship with the very One who, because of His love, died for you.

---❖---

God is always with you—every second of every single day.

One day as I was preparing a message, my teenage son Zac appeared with his stack of books and sat quietly beside me. After a few minutes of silence, I became especially aware of his presence and sensed his love. I said, "Zac, I want you to know how much it means to me that you have come to sit with me." My heart melted as he replied, "Dad, that's the reason I've come. I just want to be with you." In the same way, the great heart of our living God longs for fellowship with us.

The very thing you desire—a deep, intimate relationship with God—is available every moment of the day! The Christian life is so fresh and vibrant when we truly grasp the reality of our Lord's abiding presence.

God wants you to consciously live in His presence. Brother Lawrence wrote a little devotional book, *Practicing the Presence of God.* For a time, this monk considered the task of washing greasy dishpans in a monastery to be a chore—until he began to practice the presence of God. Then that chore became a joy and an adventure.

God is always with you—every second of every single day. But at times you might ignore His presence because you are so preoccupied with your life. Sometimes you may even forget He is with you while you are busy serving Him. God wants to live His supernatural, resurrected life in and through you. His presence makes it possible for you to be in constant communication with Him and to depend on Him in every situation.

The following acrostic, "PRESENCE," offers practical suggestions for experiencing God's presence throughout the day:

*P*roclaim your love for God by reverently beginning the day with prayer and Bible reading.

*R*ecognize God's impressions on your mind and respond accordingly.

*E*xalt God by praising and thanking Him for every blessing throughout the day.

*S*peak to Him aloud when you are alone and in your thoughts when you are in public.

*E*xpress thanks to God for having everything under control in your life.

*N*otice what God does for you throughout the day.

*C*ommit to memory meaningful scriptures.

*E*xpect God's involvement and future blessings in your life.

God will fill your heart with joy as you meditate on how much He loves you. Therefore, "always be joyful. Keep on praying. No matter what happens, always be thankful, for this is God's will for you who belong to Christ Jesus" (1 Thessalonians 5:16–18). Develop the habit of practicing the presence of God to experience the joy of His loving fellowship.

14

Confide in God

With whom do you share your deepest thoughts, concerns, and secrets? It is not difficult to speak with others about superficial issues, but to share your heart requires a closer relationship and trust.

A willingness to share our heart and innermost thoughts is important in human relationships. Because of my close relationship with Vonette, I feel comfortable sharing concerns and personal desires with her that I would never communicate to anyone else. Transparency and honesty are even more foundational to developing intimacy with God.

SHARE YOUR DEEPEST CONCERNS

God wants you to share your deepest concerns and desires with Him. Nothing you say will surprise Him. You cannot hide anything from Him. He already knows your words, your deeds, your thoughts, and your motives. But He still wants you to share them with Him.

Do not be anxious about anything, but in everything, by prayer and petition, with thanksgiving, present your requests to God. And the peace of God, which transcends all understanding, will guard your hearts and your minds in Christ Jesus.

PHILIPPIANS 4:6–7 NIV

Telling God everything will deepen your relationship with Him. He will help you deal with your concerns. As you spend time alone with Him and meditate on His Word, He will show you what to do. Have you learned to openly share the concerns of your heart with Him?

TALK WITH GOD ABOUT YOUR DEFEATS AND FAILURES

Confess sins in your life that grieve or quench the Holy Spirit.

TALK WITH GOD ABOUT YOUR HOPES AND DREAMS

Be open and honest with God. Acknowledge His incredible goodness. The Word of God promises, "Delight yourself in the LORD and He will give you the desires of your heart" (Psalm 37:4 NIV). Hold onto your desires loosely and allow God to change them if they do not fit into His plan for you.

TALK WITH GOD ABOUT YOUR OPPORTUNITIES AND PURSUITS

Involve God in your commitments. Be accountable to Him for how you invest the time, abilities, and resources He has entrusted to you. "Be careful how you live, not as fools but as those who are wise. Make the most of every opportunity for doing good in these evil days" (Ephesians 5:15–16). God's inexhaustible resources are available to help you do whatever He has called you to do (Philippians 4:13).

TALK WITH GOD ABOUT YOUR TROUBLES AND ADVERSITIES

God is working out His purposes through your difficulties to make you more like Christ. Your personal disappointments can be God's divine appointments. Ask Him what His purpose is for your problems and then cooperate with Him. Be assured your heavenly Father wants to help you.

David proclaims, "I am overcome with joy because of your unfailing love, for you have seen my troubles, and you care about the anguish of my soul" (Psalm 31:7). God understands what you are going through. As you discuss your problems with Him, He will work in your circumstances and will sovereignly use them for your good (Romans 8:28).

TALK WITH GOD ABOUT YOUR DOUBTS AND FEARS

There is no end to "what if" scenarios that predict impending disaster. But God does not want you to fear what may happen tomorrow. He wants you to cast your cares on Him today (Psalm 55:22; 1 Peter 5:7). Your loving God holds your future in His sovereign hands.

God encourages us, "Don't be afraid, for I am with you. Do not be dismayed, for I am your God. I will strengthen you. I will help you. I will uphold you with My victorious right hand" (Isaiah 41:10). Share your worries and fears with God. When you do, He will quiet your anxious heart as you are reminded of His awesome greatness and loving commitment to you.

Take time to bare your soul to God. He is waiting for you to share all your concerns with Him.

O SOVEREIGN LORD, I AM YOUR SERVANT. YOU HAVE ONLY
BEGUN TO SHOW ME YOUR GREATNESS AND POWER. IS
THERE ANY GOD IN HEAVEN OR ON EARTH WHO CAN
PERFORM SUCH GREAT DEEDS AS YOURS?

DEUTERONOMY 3:24

15

Watch God Work

When you care about a person, you notice what he does for you and you express your appreciation. When you are in love, you enjoy watching your beloved engaged in various activities.

I am impressed with Vonnette's effectiveness at everything she does—speaking at conferences, counseling, organizing events, and much more. In fact, I call her "superwife," "supermom," "supergrandma"—super everything. To be around her makes my heart beat faster. Even so, over time I have learned how easy it is to take her for granted. All too often I am so self-absorbed that I do not notice what others, even my loved ones, do around me.

God is at work in your life every day. But sadly, you may be so preoccupied with daily activities and pressures that you do not even notice or acknowledge the many things He does for you. And even when you do recognize His involvement in the circumstances of your day, it may be a fleeting moment of recognition.

David proclaimed, "Remember the wonders he has done,

his miracles, and the judgments he pronounced" (Psalm 105:5 NIV). Develop the habit of observing what God is doing in your life and in the world around you. This can be difficult because your days may be filled with activities. So many things demand your attention that you could quickly forget about the One who is always with you and sovereignly working for your benefit. Make it a habit every night to thank God for specific blessings you enjoyed that day.

God is at work in your life every day.

It is helpful to keep a written record so you will not forget special demonstrations of God's goodness and faithfulness. During your devotions, jot down a key word, phrase, or sentence as a reminder for each special thing you noticed. Your list will be a memorial like the altars biblical patriarchs built to remember what God had done for them.

Some entries may be more dramatic than others—like protection from an accident, receiving something you critically needed, or experiencing an exciting answer to a prayer. But also record little things that might seem insignificant to someone else but have special meaning to you. The item does not need to be impressive, just something that the Holy Spirit helped you notice as a sign of God's love and goodness.

Use the following questions as a practical way to observe God's involvement in your life:

- How has God recently demonstrated His love and goodness to you?
- Did you notice God controlling circumstances?
- Did God intervene to help you in a negative situation?
- Did God provide for a particular need?
- Did God protect you from harm or evil?

- Did God answer a specific prayer?
- Did God do something else that was special to you?

This routine will cause your spiritual radar to be more active throughout the day and make you especially aware of God's involvement in your life. Consequently, you will spend more time talking to Him throughout the day. And when you periodically review past entries, your faith will be greatly encouraged.

THOSE WHO KNOW YOUR NAME TRUST IN YOU,
FOR YOU, O LORD, HAVE NEVER ABANDONED
ANYONE WHO SEARCHES FOR YOU.

PSALM 9:10

16

Entrust Yourself to God's Care

Relationships of trust require a certain level of friendship and understanding. You depend on trusted friends with your precious possessions because you know they will take good care of them. You even allow close friends to handle sensitive, critical problems for you.

As you learn more about God and His attributes, your relationship with Him becomes increasingly personal and intimate. Then you will become more willing to trust Him with your problems and the things that are important to you.

God wants you to totally entrust yourself, those who are dear to you, and all that you possess to His care. Jesus told His followers, "You must put aside your selfish ambition, shoulder your cross, and follow me. If you try to keep your life for yourself, you will lose it. But if you give up your life for my sake and for the sake of the Good News, you will find true life" (Mark 8:34–35). But your willingness to do so depends on your knowledge of who He is and on your growing relationship with Him.

It is not necessary for you to write out an actual "contract" as Vonette and I did, though it has been very helpful to us. But make your act of total surrender and dedication to God a milestone event that you will never forget. Then daily remind yourself that you are not only a child of God, but as an act of your will, you have become Christ's slave, dedicated to serving Him wholeheartedly. As you encounter circumstances, concerns, or decisions throughout the day, remember that Jesus is your Master. Let Him guide you through His inspired Word and the leading of the Holy Spirit. In the process, relax and trust Him with the results.

God is worthy of your total trust. Being a servant to Christ in His kingdom will result in infinitely greater significance, fulfillment, and rewards than from any other investment of your life. Entrust yourself completely into His loving and capable care.

17

Live It!

As you grow to appreciate all that God did for you through Christ, you will increasingly desire to know Him and please Him. Your love for God will become wholehearted. And your relationship with God will deepen so that you will have a passion for the same things that God cares about.

Many years ago, a friend shared a prayer with me that I have prayed countless times since. It is simply, "Lord, give me a passion for the things that are most important to You."

Your relationship with your Creator will grow only as far as your desire permits. The Word of God promises in Psalm 34:10, "Those who trust in the LORD will never lack any good thing." As God's children we should seek Him wholeheartedly so that we can experience the intimate relationship with Him and develop a passion for His purposes.

My study of the Scriptures, my experiences in walking with our Lord since 1945, and my observation of thousands of believers around the world during the last five decades all lead me to the same conclusion: It is absolute folly for a Christian to live even one split second out of the perfect will of God. You can never be satisfied with living a mediocre Christian life. The privilege of knowing, loving, and serving your gracious God and Savior is so awesome that to sacrifice this for any pleasure—money, sex, power, fame—is ludicrous. Nothing compares to the abundant, supernatural life Christ wants to live in and through you.

> *It is absolute folly for a Christian to live even one split second out of the perfect will of God.*

Where are you in your relationship with God? What changes does God want you to make so you will develop wholehearted passion for Him? What steps can you take today and this week?

Only by completely trusting your life to God can you accomplish anything of eternal value. Only by daily placing your faith in Him can you experience supernatural living. He is the reason you were born, and He is the one who has opened the door of eternity to you. He has offered you intimacy. Are you seeking Him wholeheartedly?

Readers' Guide

For Personal Reflection
or Group Discussion

Questions are an inevitable part of life. Proud parents ask their new baby, "Can you smile?" Later they ask, "Can you say 'Mama'?" "Can you walk to Daddy?" The early school years bring the inevitable, "What did you learn at school today?" Later school years introduce tougher questions, "If X equals 12 and Y equals –14, then …?" Adulthood adds a whole new set of questions. "Should I remain single or marry?" "How did things go at the office?" "Did you get a raise?" "Should we let Susie start dating?" "Which college is right for Kyle?" "How can we possibly afford to send our kids to college?"

This book raises questions, too. The following study guide is designed to: (1) maximize the subject material and (2) apply biblical truth to daily life. You won't be asked to solve any algebraic problems or recall dates associated with obscure events in history, so relax. Questions asking for objective information are based solely on the text. Most questions, however, prompt you to search inside your soul, examine the circumstances that surround your life, and decide how you can best use the truths communicated in the book.

Honest answers to real issues can strengthen your faith, draw you closer to the Lord, and lead you into fuller, richer, more joyful, and productive daily adventure. So confront each question head-on and expect the One who is the Answer for all of life's questions and needs to accomplish great things in your life.

CHAPTER 1: WANDERING, NOT LOST

1. Do you agree that the world's greatest need is love? Defend your answer.

2. What kind of neighbor is the hardest to love? How can a believer show genuine love to such a neighbor?

3. If a Christian no longer loves the Lord as he or she did when first saved, what do you think went wrong?

4. How does a believer's wandering from his or her first love for the Lord affect God's love for that believer?

5. How can a wandering believer's first love for the Lord be restored?

CHAPTER 2: TRANSFORMED BY LOVE

1. How did God's love take Dr. Bright by surprise? Did it take you by surprise? If so, how?

2. How can you tell the difference between real love and feigned love?

3. The author speaks about "the Fellowship of the Burning Heart." If you had to decide on membership in this fellowship, what criteria would you apply?

4. How is it possible that work for God may shut out real love for God?

5. If you could invite Martha's sister Mary into your home for a chat, what would you say to her? What do you think she would say to you?

CHAPTER 3: REMEMBRANCE: RELIVING YOUR FIRST LOVE

1. Why is the mind "the best place to stir up the embers that will warm your heart once again"?

2. How might a lukewarm Christian sense God's call to a renewed love for Him?

3. What does it say about one's love for God if the desire to spend time with Him is absent? Why does a Christian who loves God want to spend time with Him?

4. How are the dynamics of a good marriage similar to a loving relationship with God?

5. What might some believers try to substitute for real love for God? If you could offer one sentence of advice to Christians who have left their first love, what would it be?

CHAPTER 4: REMORSE: REALIZING THE LOSS

1. Have you seen evidence of "godly sorrow" recently? If not, do you think it has not been necessary, or do you think it has been ignored? Explain.

2. What is one benefit of "good pain" in regard to godly sorrow?

3. What kinds of pain does the author compare to the pain of godly sorrow? What can you add to his list?

4. What pitfalls should a believer watch out for if he or she wants to enjoy a loving relationship with God?

5. How is returning to one's first love similar to coming home after a long, disappointing absence?

CHAPTER 5: REPENTANCE: REMOVING THE OBSTACLES

1. What does it mean to repent? Do you think Christians generally view repentance as a negative act? What might it take to change this erroneous concept?

2. How does the author link "Spiritual Breathing" to the act of repenting?

3. Why do you agree or disagree that fasting is a prerequisite to national revival?

4. How does prayer jump-start repentance?

5. What items belong on what Dr. Bright calls your "turn-around list"?

CHAPTER 6: RESUMPTION: REJOINING THE PATH OF OBEDIENCE

1. How does the author use the word *resume* to refer to godly sorrow?

2. What situations have you seen turn around in sports because a team or player returned to the basics?

3. What do you see as the basics of Christian living?

4. How hard is it to love those who hurt us? How can we obey the command to love our fellow believers?

5. How does ego act as a big foe when we attempt to love those who hurt us?

CHAPTER 7: REVIVAL: REJOICING IN THE LIGHT

1. What image portrayed in the parable of the prodigal son do you find most amazing? Why?

2. Why might some Christians have a negative image of God, the Father?

3. How might you correct this faulty image for a misguided Christian?

4. What does it say about God's love that He forgave David's sin of adultery and restored His joy to David? What emotions did David experience before receiving this forgiveness?

5. How can you tell that a believer's heart burns with love for God?

CHAPTER 8: REWARD: RESTING IN THE SHADE OF ETERNITY

1. What does it mean to "overcome" as a believer?

2. How does a believer become an overcomer?

3. Why is the love of God essential to spiritual productivity?

4. Comparing your Christian experience to tree roots, how well rooted are you? What would it take to grow stronger roots?

5. Why is heaven such a wonderful place? How eagerly are you anticipating heaven?

CHAPTER 9: AN INVITATION TO INTIMACY WITH GOD

1. How is it possible for sinful human beings to have fellowship with a holy God?

2. How did God communicate with humankind through Jesus Christ?

3. What life-changes does the Holy Spirit effect in the Christian's life?

4. What does it mean to seek God wholeheartedly?

5. How can your best human relationship help you understand how to seek God wholeheartedly?

CHAPTER 10: DESIRE INTIMACY WITH GOD

1. What part does desire play in a relationship?

2. How do you feel when someone rejects your love? Do you think God feels the same way when people reject His love? Why or why not?

3. How can a believer make the most of the time spent with God?

4. Why is thirsting for water such a good analogy of thirsting for God?

5. How can you increase your thirst for God?

CHAPTER 11: RESPECT GOD AND HIS RULES

1. Have you ever found yourself in a disagreement with God? Who was at fault? How was the disagreement resolved?

2. Why is obedience to Jesus' commandments a test of love for Him?

3. Why does God deserve our greatest respect and highest honor? How can believers show Him proper respect and honor?

4. How do small sins have a way of evolving into big sins?

5. What actions can a believer take to stay pure?

CHAPTER 12: UNDERSTAND GOD BETTER

1. In what sense is the Bible inspired?

2. Why did God give us the Bible?

3. Do you agree or disagree that a lack of familiarity with the Bible causes a lack of understanding of God? Defend your answer.

4. How does one's understanding of God affect his or her lifestyle?

5. Beginning now, what steps will you take to better your understanding of God?

CHAPTER 13: ENJOY GOD'S PRESENCE

1. How is it possible to enjoy God's presence at the workplace?

2. Is God closer to us at church than elsewhere? Explain.

3. How can you talk to God while driving a car or sitting in a doctor's office or anywhere?

4. What synonyms for "fellowship" with God might enhance its meaning?

5. How can you practice the presence of God?

CHAPTER 14: CONFIDE IN GOD

1. What deep thoughts and desires have you shared with God recently?

2. How does it make you feel to know that God wants you to share your deepest thoughts and desires with Him?

3. Why should a believer confide in God?

4. Why doesn't it make good sense to try to hide our thoughts and desires from God?

5. What defeats and failures do you need to confess to God? What positive results will this confession bring?

CHAPTER 15: WATCH GOD WORK

1. What evidence of God's working in the lives of His people have you observed?

2. How is God working in your life?

3. How can believers show appreciation for God's work in their lives?

4. How can a daily record help believers focus on God's goodness and faithfulness? What kinds of things should such a record include?

5. What are a few of the questions Dr. Bright poses to help believers recognize God's wonderful works on their behalf?

CHAPTER 16: ENTRUST YOURSELF TO GOD'S CARE

1. What kinds of problems do believers sometimes fail to entrust to God?

2. Why are we so slow to commit our burdens to the Lord?

3. Dr. Bright cites a "contract" with God that he and his wife drafted. Do you agree or disagree that such a commitment might be a good idea for every Christian? Why or why not?

4. What do you think total commitment to the Lord involves?

5. What rewards come to those who trust God with all they are and possess?

CHAPTER 17: LIVE IT!

1. Read Hebrews 11:24–26. How does this passage agree with Dr. Bright's belief that nothing compares with the life Christ offers?

2. What changes might you make this week to follow Christ wholeheartedly?

3. Why is God's will vastly superior to self-will?

4. What are some things every Christian should want to accomplish during life's pilgrimage?

5. How will you deepen your intimacy with God this week?

Appendix

God's Word on Intimacy with Him

Following are selected Scripture references that were presented throughout the text of this book. We encourage you to sit down with your Bible and review these verses in their context, prayerfully reflecting upon what God's Word tells you about the joy of intimacy with Him.

CHAPTER 1
Romans 8:38–39
1 Corinthians
  13:1–3
1 John 4:16
Galatians 2:20
1 Thessalonians
  5:17
Job 1:21
Galatians 5:16–17
1 Corinthians 13:13

CHAPTER 2
1 John 4:10–19

Philippians 2:7
2 Peter 1:1
James 1:1
Jude 1
Philippians 4:19
Luke 10:38–42
Matthew 6:33
Matthew 13:22
Revelation 2:2–5
Mark 12:30–31
John 15:4
Matthew 28:20
2 Chronicles 7:14
Revelation 2:7

CHAPTER 3
Revelation 2:5a

CHAPTER 4
2 Corinthians
  7:9–10
Luke 15:11–32

CHAPTER 5
Revelation 2:5b
John 8:12
Galatians 5:16–17
1 John 1:9
Ephesians 5:18
1 John 5:14–15

Psalm 51:7–8
Psalm 32:1–6

CHAPTER 6
Revelation 2:5c
Revelation 2:2
1 John 4:19
Philippians 2:13
Luke 10:27
John 13:34–35
Matthew 5:44

CHAPTER 7
Luke 15
Isaiah 62:5
Psalm 51:10, 12
1 John 1:7

CHAPTER 8
Revelation 2:7
1 Corinthians
    13:12

CHAPTER 9
Matthew 22:37
Job 33:4
Acts 17:25
Romans 14:11
Romans 10:9
John 1:12–13
Isaiah 61:10
2 Corinthians 5:2
John 1:1, 14
John 14:9
1 John 1:1–2
1 John 5:20

1 John 4:13
Galatians 4:6
John 14:16, 17
Romans 5:5
John 6:63
1 Corinthians 2:10
Romans 8:26–27
Jeremiah 29:13

CHAPTER 10
1 Chronicles 28:9
Matthew 22:37
John 14:23
Psalm 63:1–3
Matthew 6:33

CHAPTER 11
John 14:21
John 5:30
Isaiah 26:8–9
Psalm 25:14
Psalm 147:11
Psalm 66:18
Hebrews 12:5–11
1 John 1:9

CHAPTER 12
Ephesians 1:16–17
John 6:63
Hebrews 4:12
Psalm 119:105
Ephesians 6:17
Luke 8:11, 15
Philippians 3:8

CHAPTER 13
Psalm 16:8
2 Corinthians 6:16
1 Corinthians 3:16
Isaiah 41:13
Deuteronomy 31:6
1 Thessalonians
    5:16–18

CHAPTER 14
Philippians 4:6–7
Psalm 37:4
Ephesians 5:15–16
Philippians 4:13
Psalm 31:7
Romans 8:28
Psalm 55:22
1 Peter 5:7
Isaiah 41:10

CHAPTER 15
Deuteronomy 3:24
Psalm 105:5

CHAPTER 16
Psalm 9:10
Philippians 2:5–8
Romans 1:1
Mark 8:34–35

CHAPTER 17
Psalm 34:10

About the Author

DR. BILL BRIGHT, fueled by his passion to share the love and claims of Jesus Christ with "every living person on earth," was the founder and president of Campus Crusade for Christ. The world's largest Christian ministry, Campus Crusade serves people in 191 countries through a staff of 26,000 full-time employees and more than 225,000 trained volunteers working in some sixty targeted ministries and projects that range from military ministry to inner-city ministry.

Bill Bright was so motivated by what is known as the Great Commission, Christ's command to carry the gospel throughout the world, that in 1956 he wrote a booklet titled *The Four Spiritual Laws*, which has been printed in 200 languages and distributed to more than 2.5 billion people. Other books Bright authored include *Discover the Book God Wrote, God: Discover His Character, Come Help Change Our World, The Holy Spirit: The Key to Supernatural Living, Life Without Equal, Witnessing Without Fear, Coming Revival, Journey Home,* and *Red Sky in the Morning.*

In 1979 Bright commissioned the *JESUS* film, a feature-length dramatization of the life of Christ. To date, the film has been viewed by more than 5.7 billion people in 191 countries and has become the most widely viewed and translated film in history.

Dr. Bright died in July 2003 before the final editing of this book. But he prayed that it would leave a legacy of his love for Jesus and the power of the Holy Spirit to change lives. He is survived by his wife, Vonette; their sons and daughters-in-law; and four grandchildren.